Quirky CARDIFF

MARK REES

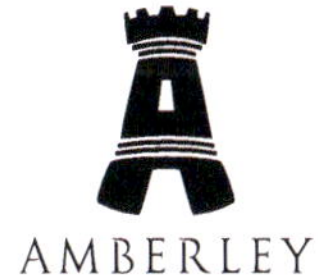

AMBERLEY

First published 2026

Amberley Publishing
The Hill, Stroud
Gloucestershire, GL5 4EP

www.amberley-books.com

British Library Cataloguing in Publication Data.
A catalogue record for this book is available from the British Library.

ISBN 978 1 3981 2241 3 (paperback)
ISBN 978 1 3981 2242 0 (ebook)

Typesetting by SJmagic DESIGN SERVICES, India.
Printed in Great Britain.

Appointed GPSR EU Representative:
Easy Access System Europe Oü, 16879218
Address: Mustamäe tee 50, 10621, Tallinn, Estonia
Contact Details: gpsr.requests@easproject.com, +358 40 500 3575

Contents

Introduction

The word 'quirky' is, in and of itself, a little bit quirky.

How do you define it? According to the Oxford Thesaurus, it is an adjective that means 'eccentric, idiosyncratic, unconventional, unorthodox, unusual, off-centre, strange, bizarre, peculiar, odd, outlandish, zany'. More informally, it means 'wacky, freaky, kinky, way-out, far out, kooky, offbeat'.

When it comes to defining a book like *Quirky Cardiff*, these words serve as a pretty good starting point. This is an unconventional – to use one of the words suggested – journey through the history of the city, focussing on the lesser-known facts and overlooked features. While it does include some of the major events and figures from Cardiff's past, it does so in an unorthodox – another one of the words suggested – manner.

Quirky Cardiff shines a light on some of the eccentric characters, strange works of art, and offbeat curiosities that have long hidden in plain sight. Even if some of the names and places seem very familiar, it will still, I hope, reveal some surprising facts. For example, while most people are aware that Dame Shirley Bassey was born and raised in the parish, did you know that her long-demolished birthplace is now identifiable by a marker in the pavement?

A key aspect of this book is the images, and the dozens of entries that made the final cut have been chosen because, in many cases, they can be visited today. Some continue as if time has stood still, such as the room where Captain Scott and his crew filled their stomachs with a farewell feast before setting sail on their ill-fated journey. Even those locations that might have changed beyond recognition often leave clues behind that offer hints at their previous lives.

To reflect these varied aspects of the book, it has been divided into seven chapters. Each one focusses on a different characteristic of the city's past, ensuring a nice balance between subjects and a consistent tone – for every account of a grisly murder, there's a light-hearted tale to counterbalance it.

The first chapter, 'Only in Cardiff', explores the things that make Cardiff unique and, frankly, don't really fit anywhere else – they really show Cardiff at its quirkiest. 'Scars of History' takes a chronological look at how the past has shaped the present, while 'Famous Faces' examines some of the people who put Cardiff on the map, but not necessarily the most obvious names.

This ties in nicely with the following chapter, 'Capital of Culture', in which Cardiff's superpower as a crucible for the arts is highlighted, followed by 'Law and Order', which examines the city's darker underbelly with some famous and not-so-famous criminal deeds from days gone by. The penultimate chapter, 'Weird and Wonderful', is, as the name suggests, is the most unconventional of chapters, delving into the more uncanny accounts of UFOs, poltergeists and vampires.

Finally, we wrap things up with the twin subjects that, for many people, define a visit to Cardiff, 'Sport and Nightlife'. Because if you really want to know Cardiff, then you have to know the Cardiff people, and what better way of doing so than roaring on your local team in the stadium before heading down Chippy Lane at the end of a good day or night out?

Mark Rees, 2026

Only in Cardiff

All cities have their own quirky characteristics that set them apart. Each one has its own unique history, architecture, and colourful characters unlikely to be found in nearby towns. Cardiff, the capital of Wales, exemplifies this with an abundance of intriguing features. Caerdydd, to give it its Welsh language name, has been a dynamic hub of industry and culture for centuries, and this rich history has left a legacy of curiosities that now adorn its streets.

For instance, what does the Cardiff coat of arms signify? Why is there a lion perched atop a building in the middle of the city? And did the first million-pound cheque really get signed in the Coal Exchange? These are just a few of the questions that reveal Cardiff's unique charm.

In this first chapter we'll go in search of some of these unusual and at times unlikely treasures – those features that locals might pass by every day without ever stopping to consider their origins or significance.

Cardiff's Coat of Arms

Cardiff's coat of arms is a familiar sight in the city. It can be seen most prominently outside City Hall, and if it's a match day, you might see the arms proudly emblazoned on the front of a retro Cardiff City FC shirt. But beyond simply representing the city, what does it actually mean?

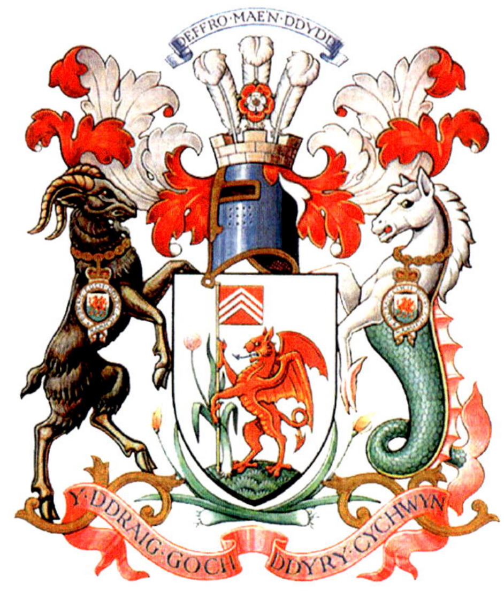

Coat of arms of Cardiff. (© Ashley0690 (Wikimedia, CC BY-SA 3.0))

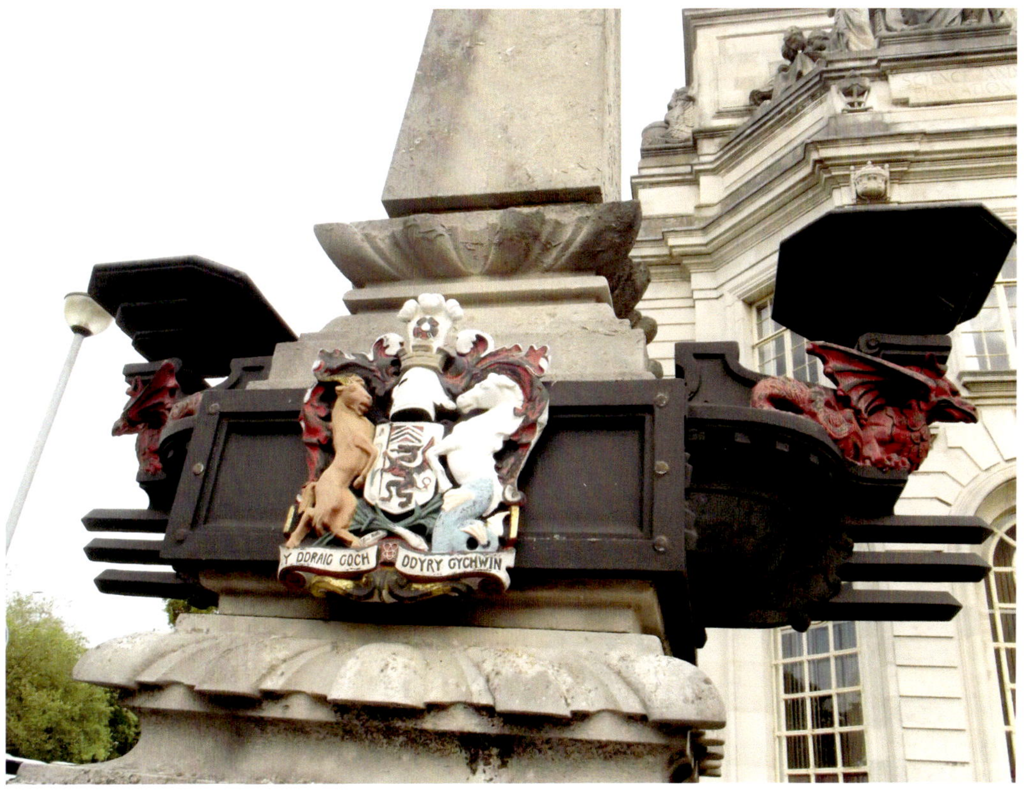

Cardiff Crown Court. (© Elliott Brown (Flickr, CC BY-SA 2.0))

The arms themselves date from 1906, and the complete coat of arms was exemplified in 1956, the year after Cardiff was declared the capital city of Wales. Having been readopted by the council in 1996, it became a permanent reminder of the city's prominent status, and this is reflected in the iconography.

Central to the arms is the red dragon (y ddraig goch), the emblem of Wales, which is shown holding aloft a red standard featuring three white chevrons. The chevrons have been attributed to Iestyn ap Gwrgant, the last ruler of Morgannwg (Glamorgan) who resided in Cardiff Castle in the eleventh century, and later become the arms of the subsequent Lords of Glamorgan and Cardiff. The leeks and the daffodils, along with the motto beneath the shield, 'Y ddraig goch ddyry cychwyn' (the red dragon will lead the way), reinforce Cardiff's role as the capital of Wales.

The crest surrounding the arms underscores loyalty to the Crown, pays homage to the city's ancient traditions, and highlights how Cardiff bridges the mountains and the seas. On one side stands a Welsh goat, an ancient emblem of the mountains, while a hippocamp, or seahorse, representing the surrounding seas and Cardiff's bustling port trade, stands on the other. The crest is adorned with a Tudor rose, the symbol of the House of Tudor, the dynasty of Welsh descent that held the throne of England, and three ostrich feathers, another royal link that suggests the heraldic badge of the Prince of Wales. A second motto above the feathers aims to rouse the residents to be ever alert and vigilant: 'Deffro mae'n ddydd' (Awake, it is day).

The Lion of St Mary Street

You might not have noticed it before – in which case you'll be amazed at how you managed to miss it – but keeping a close eye on the hustle and bustle of city life on St Mary Street is a life-size statue of a lion. Yes, if you look up, there's a giant sculpture of the king of the jungle perched on top of the Sandringham Hotel, the origins of which hark back to the early days of the building.

Built in the 1880s and established as a hotel in 1892, the building was originally known as the Black Lion, hence the maned predator sitting on high, and was a favoured destination for farmers and tradesmen who needed some entertainment after a hard day's work. It continued to be a popular watering hole well into the twentieth century, and in 1989, the hotel was taken over by the Dutton family, led by local favourite Eric Dutton, who was awarded an MBE in 2003 for over fifty years of voluntary service to the Cardiff community. Following a name

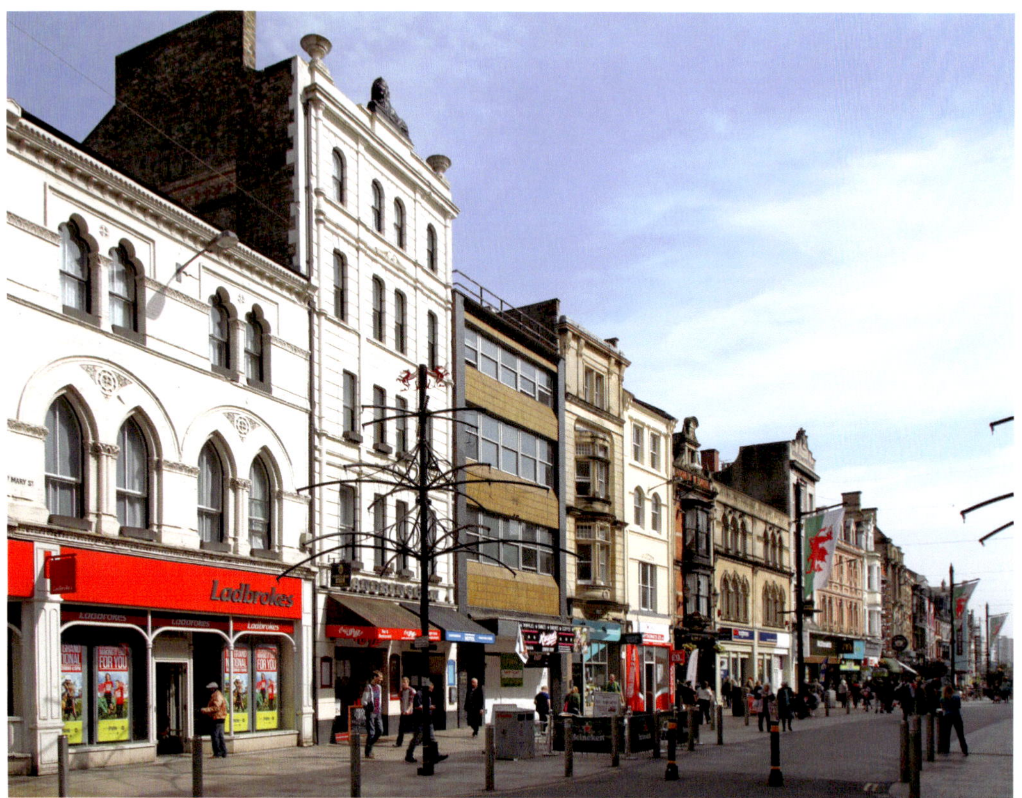

The lion looks down from the Sandringham Hotel. (© Allie_Caulfield (Flickr, CC BY 2.0))

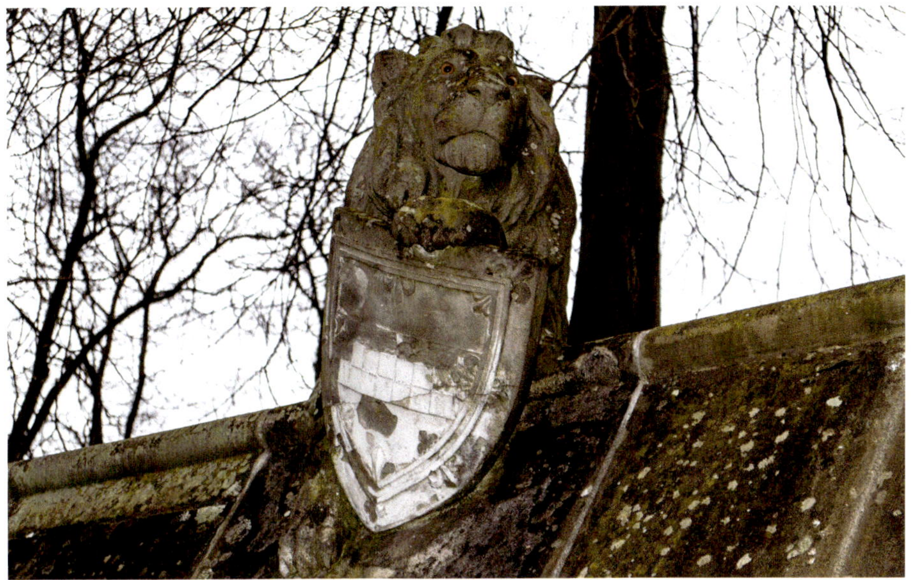

One of the lions keeping watch on the Animal Wall. (© MrsEllacott (Wikimedia, CC BY-SA 3.0))

change, it developed a reputation as a go-to place for jazz fans, with the dedicated Café Jazz welcoming musicians from around the world.

Fans of lion statues can find even more on the nearby Cardiff Castle Animal Wall that runs along Castle Street. Dotted with stone animals, there is also a hyena, seal, apes, wolf, bear, lynx, vulture, beaver, leopard, raccoon, anteater, and a pelican.

The First £1 Million Cheque?

It has long been claimed that the world's 'first £1 million cheque' was signed in Cardiff. Something of an urban myth in the city, according to the story it was signed in the iconic Coal Exchange building, or the Coal and Shipping Exchange as it was originally known, following a major deal in 1904.

Completed in 1886 and officially opened in 1888, the Coal Exchange played a pivotal role in the global coal trade. While it has had many ups and downs over the years, its eye-catching Renaissance Revival style has made it an ever-popular photogenic landmark, even when the doors have been closed to the public. In its heyday, this architectural gem served as the bustling trading floor for coal owners and ship agents. The peak trading hour could witness chaotic scenes of up to 200 people frantically overseeing and finalising agreements, with wild gesturing and the sounds of frantic exchanges filling the air. It was during the time of such scenes that the £1 million cheque deal is said to have taken place.

Sadly, there is no known evidence to support the claim. It was certainly not reported in 1904 when the events are said to have taken place, and only emerged

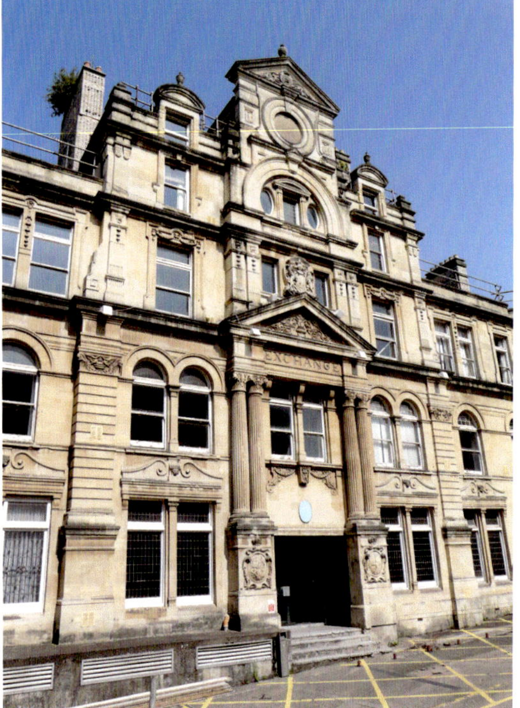

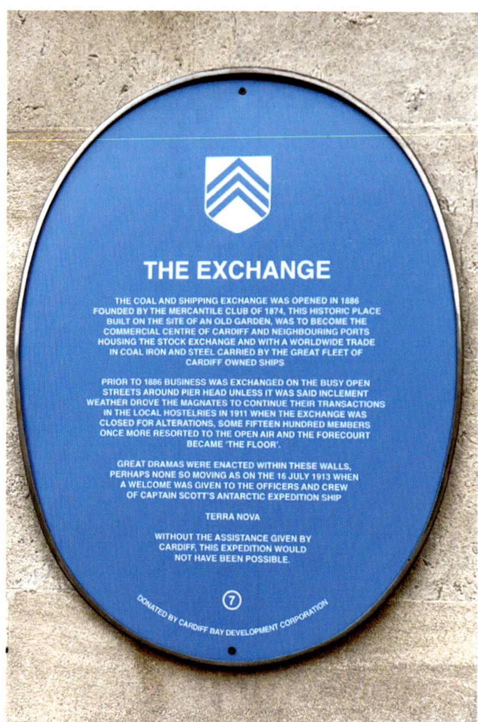

Above left: The Coal Exchange. (© Ham (Wikimedia, CC BY-SA 3.0 DEED))

Above right: The blue plaque outside the Coal Exchange. (© Ferdi2005 (Wikimedia, CC BY-SA 4.0))

in the press several years later. While it is very possible that a £1 million deal might have been made in the Coal Exchange, the key factor is the cheque. In the absence of any concrete evidence – which at this stage is unlikely to be found – it cannot be confirmed. Doubt will continue to be cast on the claim, and it will simply remain a quirky Cardiff story.

The Coal Exchange has many other claims to fame besides the tale of the cheque, and a blue plaque on the entrance to the building reads: 'Great dramas were enacted within these walls, perhaps none so moving as on the 16 July 1913 when a welcome was given to the officers and crew of Captain Scott's Antarctic expedition ship Terra Nova. Without the assistance given by Cardiff, this expedition would not have been possible.' As shall be revealed later in this book, this wasn't the only place in Cardiff with a connection to that celebrated, if ill-fated, voyage.

The First Broadcast in Wales

Anyone arriving in Cardiff by train today can't fail to notice BBC Cymru Wales's broadcasting house. Standing on the site of the former central bus station, the

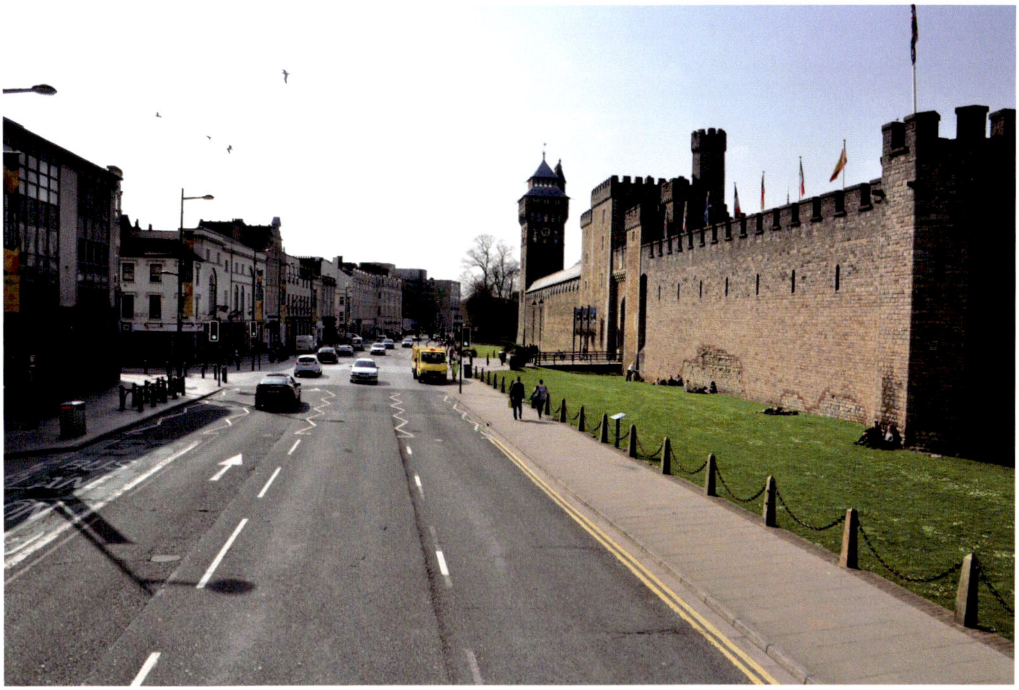

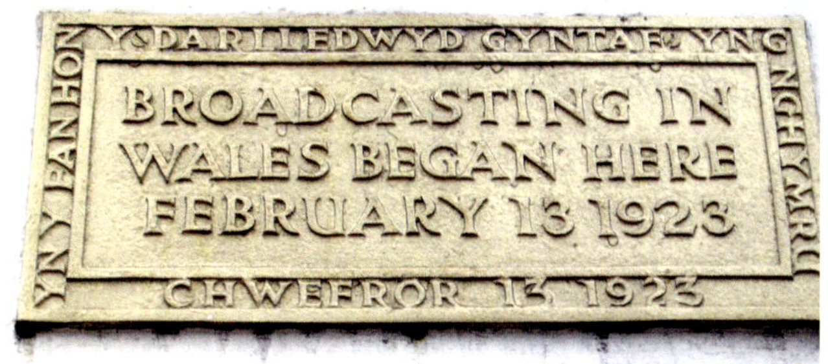

Above: Cardiff Street.
(© Lewis Clarke
(Wikimedia, CC BY-SA 2.0))

Right: The plaque
commemorating the
first broadcast in
Wales. (© Seth Whales
(Wikimedia, CC BY-SA 3.0))

custom-built building looms over Central Square, a glistening modern tower block in the heart of the city. Housing the nation's public broadcaster since it opened its doors to staff in 2019, it's a far cry from the early days of radio in both Wales and Cardiff, which began in more humble circumstances a short walk away.

It was at No. 19 Castle Street, a building that now proudly displays a plaque commemorating the occasion, that the BBC's Cardiff station 5WA – with 5 being its station number, and WA referring to its location in Wales – beamed out its first broadcast, at 5 p.m. on 13 February 1923. With an aerial at Eldon Street, it began with an hour of children's storytelling, followed by the Wireless Orchestra's rendition of Julius Fučík's *Entry of the Gladiators*, a tune best known today for its association with clowns and circuses. A series of speeches followed from prominent members of the BBC, including the reading of a message from former Prime Minister David Lloyd George, and the mayor of Cardiff, Dr. J. J. E. Biggs, who declared the station open at 7 p.m. He was thrilled that from that day forth 'the highest form of culture will be taken into the homes of the poorest in the land'.

Following an hour or two of news and weather reports, at 9.30 p.m. renowned operatic baritone Mostyn Thomas sang the Welsh language folk song 'Dafydd y Garreg Wen' (David of the White Rock), the first Welsh language song to be publicly broadcast in Wales. The first Welsh language talk would follow soon after on the same channel on St David's Day. This balance between English and Welsh language output eventually led to the establishment of a second station dedicated solely to the Welsh language, BBC Radio Cymru, in 1977. The English-language BBC Radio Wales followed in 1978, both of which are still going strong today.

The Pillar Box-Eating Tree

One of Cardiff's most beloved, and arguably quirkiest, landmarks can be found on Ninian Road in Roath: a Grade II listed Royal Mail pillar box that, over the

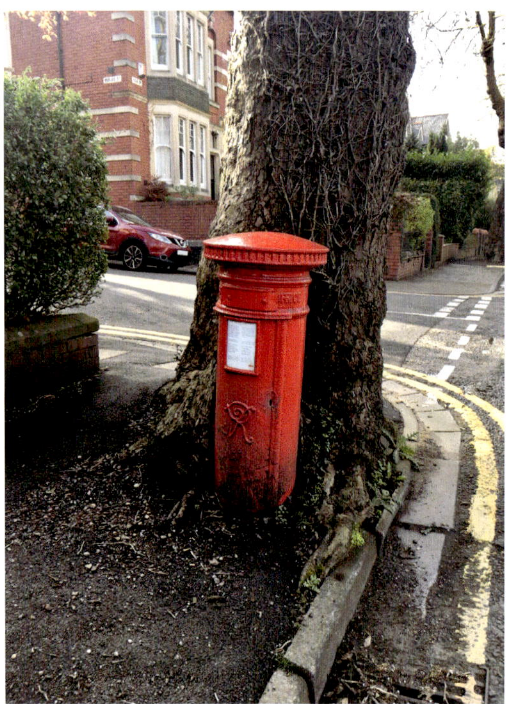

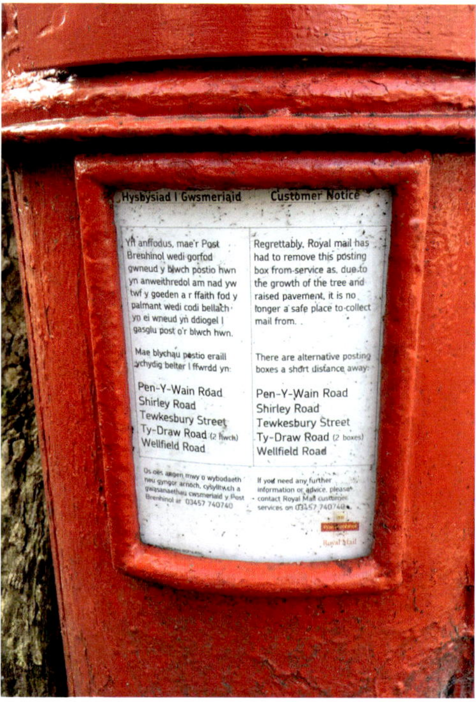

Above left: The pillar box on Ninian Road. (© No Swan So Fine (Wikimedia, CC BY-SA 4.0))

Above right: Detail of the pillar box sign. (© No Swan So Fine (Wikimedia, CC BY-SA 4.0))

course of a century, has succumbed to nature and is now permanently a part of the sprawling roots of an enormous tree. In fact, so consumed is it by the London plane tree that it is no longer fit to fulfil its original purpose. After more than 100 years on the job, it was officially decommissioned in 2016 by Royal Mail, who sealed the post box after deeming it unsafe for mail collection.

In what might be seen as a symbolic victory for nature – and an aesthetic victory for the locals – both the tree and the much-loved box will remain in place, despite being out of use. As a listed structure, the pillar box is a long-standing piece of the area's heritage, while the tree has grown on the spot since the turn of the twentieth century, serving as a permanent reminder of the onward march of time.

A sign on the box explains its retirement, citing safety concerns amid the tree's growth and the altered pavement level: 'Regrettably, Royal Mail has had to remove this posting box from service as, due to the growth of the tree and the raised pavement, it is no longer a safe place to collect mail from. There are alternative posting boxes a short distance away.' The nearest posting box at the time of closing was less than half a mile away.

Billy the Seal

Cardiff's most beloved non-human resident passed away in 1939, but the legacy of Billy the Seal endures to this day through sculpture, exhibitions, and the social history of the city.

Billy's tale begins in 1912 when the adventurous seal was accidentally caught in a fishing net off the coast of Ireland. Transported to Cardiff docks with the

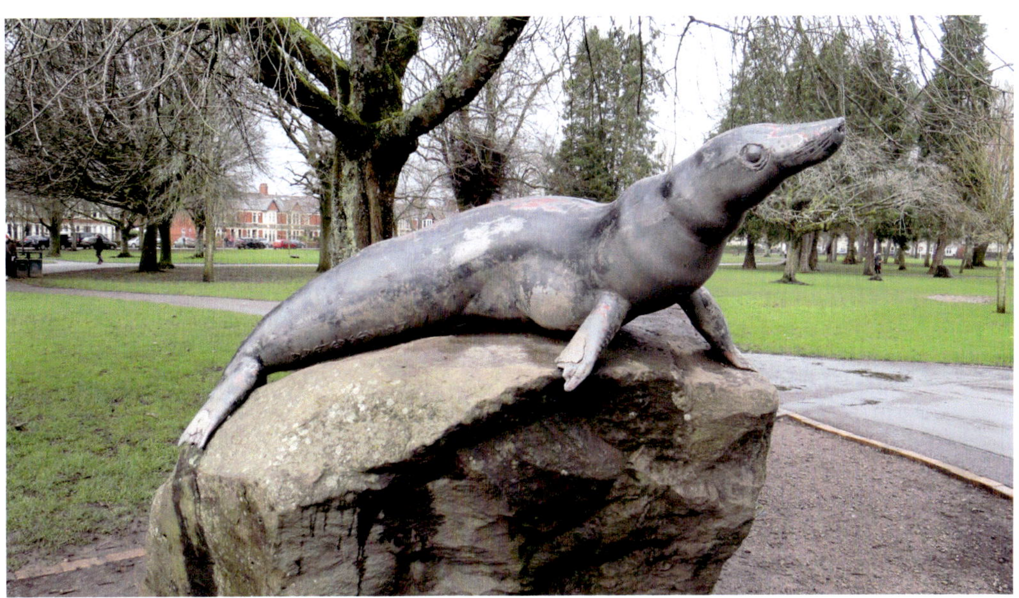

Billy the Seal. (© Ben Salter (Flickr, CC BY 2.0))

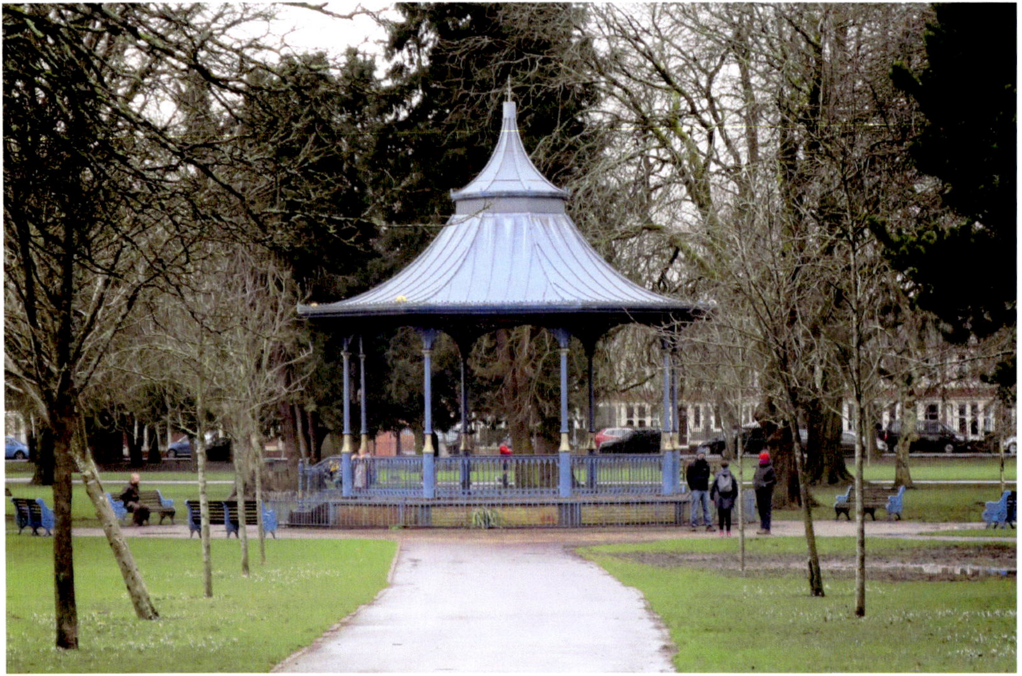

Victoria Park. (© Ben Salter (Flickr, CC BY 2.0))

day's catch, the sea animal soon found a new permanent home in Victoria Park, captivating the public with playful antics for more than two decades.

After Billy's passing, experts at National Museum Wales made a surprising discovery that further endeared 'him' to the people of Cardiff – Billy was not a 'he' as had been assumed but a 'she'. This revelation added an intriguing twist to her tale, and in 2010 her skeleton made a triumphant return to the public eye as a prominent feature in a new gallery at the museum.

Today, a bronze sculpture of Billy, created by Cardiff-born sculptor David Petersen in 1997, can be found next to the paddling pool in the park where she first found fame. While the pool has undergone significant upgrades since Billy's time, much of Victoria Park, which is named after Queen Victoria and was established to celebrate her Diamond Jubilee, retains its original charm, such as the tennis courts and a replica of the Victorian cast-iron bandstand. There have also been more recent additions, such as our next entry …

The *After Life* Bench

In 2022, Victoria Park received a new park bench which, in and of itself, isn't particularly newsworthy. It was a plain, simple bench designed purely to do what park benches do best – allow people to take the weight off their feet as they stretch their legs outdoors. What makes this bench different from the park's other benches, however, is that it was donated by Netflix to mark the poignant and prominent role such a bench plays in the final series of one of the streaming service's most consistently watched shows.

The series in question is *After Life*, the multiple award-winning comedy created, written, directed by, and starring Ricky Gervais. Twenty-five similar benches were installed across the UK, from London to Liverpool, but this is the only After Life bench to be found in Wales. Inscribed with the message 'Hope is Everything', the bench aims to shed light on themes of bereavement, loneliness, and mental health, as explored in the series. An accompanying plaque acknowledges Netflix's donation and highlights their partnership with Campaign Against Living Miserably (CALM), a suicide prevention charity that provides support, advice, and information to those struggling with mental health issues.

Gervais told the BBC: 'We hope the benches will create a lasting legacy for *After Life*, as well as become a place for people to visit.' This means fans of the series, or anyone else looking for a place of solace, are welcome to take a seat in Cardiff's Grade II listed park and enjoy the nearby flower borders on a bench that aims to do much more than provide a place to sit.

Platform Zero

Train commuters, as a rule, probably don't spend much time thinking about platform numbers. Whether you're a daily traveller dashing to the office or a

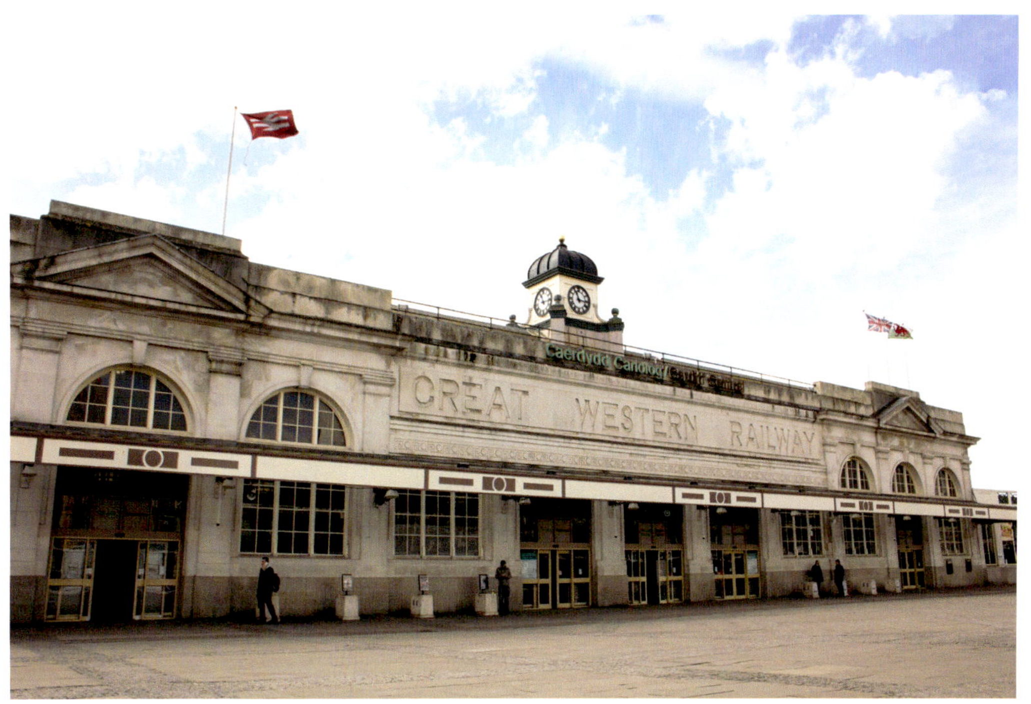

Cardiff Central station. (© Jeremy Segrott (Flickr, CC BY 2.0))

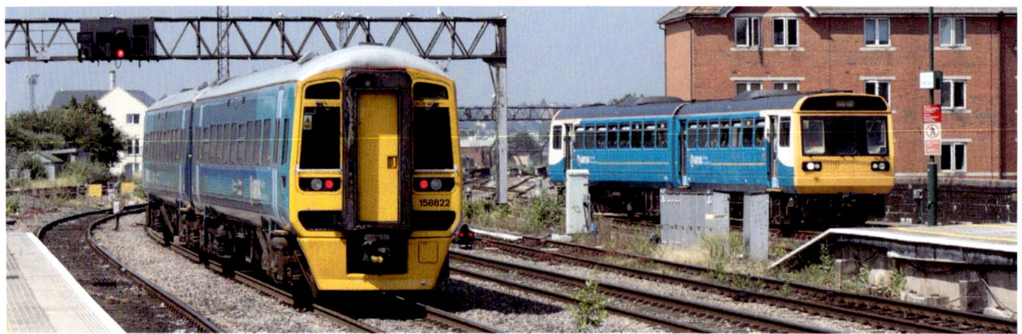

Trains passing at Cardiff Central. (© Joshua Brown (Flickr, CC BY-SA 2.0))

holidaymaker stepping foot in Cardiff for the first time, your main concerns are things like buying a ticket, finding your train, and maybe picking up a coffee to swig along the way. But when you stop to think about it, isn't it strange that Cardiff Central has a platform zero? Wouldn't it make more sense to start with platform one? And now that we're on the subject of platform numbers, why is there no platform five when there's a platform six, seven, and eight?

To answer those questions, we need to take a look at the history of Cardiff Central, a Grade II listed building that first opened in 1850. It has been known by several names over the years, switching from Cardiff station to Cardiff General in 1924, and to its current title in 1973. The distinctive Art Deco building as we see it today is a rebuild from the 1930s, undertaken by the Great Western Railway whose name is carved prominently on the façade – far more prominently than the name of the station, which is just above.

During this time, Cardiff has grown from an industrial town into a flourishing capital city, and the greater number of visitors has meant a greater number of trains and a greater number of train platforms. There are currently eight platforms that are numbered zero to four and six to eight, and the reasons there is a number zero and a missing number five relate to historical changes made over the centuries.

The easiest one to explain is platform five, which used to be a west-facing platform until it was removed in the 1960s. Two new platforms have been added since then, but it was decided not to reallocate the number as it would cause confusion having a platform five after platform seven. As such, when platform eight was introduced in 2011 as part of a major regeneration scheme, it simply took the number that followed the platform next to it.

Platform zero, on the other hand, was not so simple. Added in 1999, it has become an important through platform for additional capacity during major events and could have claimed either numbers five or eight at the time. Its position within the station, however, was unlike any of the other platforms that are reached by stairs or lifts. This smaller scale platform is accessed directly via the concourse and numbering it among the others could easily lead to misunderstandings, and so platform zero was born.

As unusual as it might sound, Cardiff is not unique in having a platform numbered zero, with a handful of others in the UK including Edinburgh's Haymarket, London's King's Cross, and Leeds railway station.

The Legacy of Shand House

Frances Batty Shand was a Victorian woman driven by a fervent desire to improve society. Her work has touched the lives of countless individuals, and while she might not be the household name she deserves to be, more than a century after her passing, one of Cardiff's most historic buildings stands as testament to her legacy.

Born in Jamaica in 1815, Shand's early life was far from easy. Her father was a Scottish plantation owner, her mother was a freed slave, and Shand was sent to live in Scotland at an early age. It was only when she moved to Cardiff in 1857 that she discovered her true calling after witnessing the hardships faced by the blind on the streets of an industrial city ill-equipped for their needs.

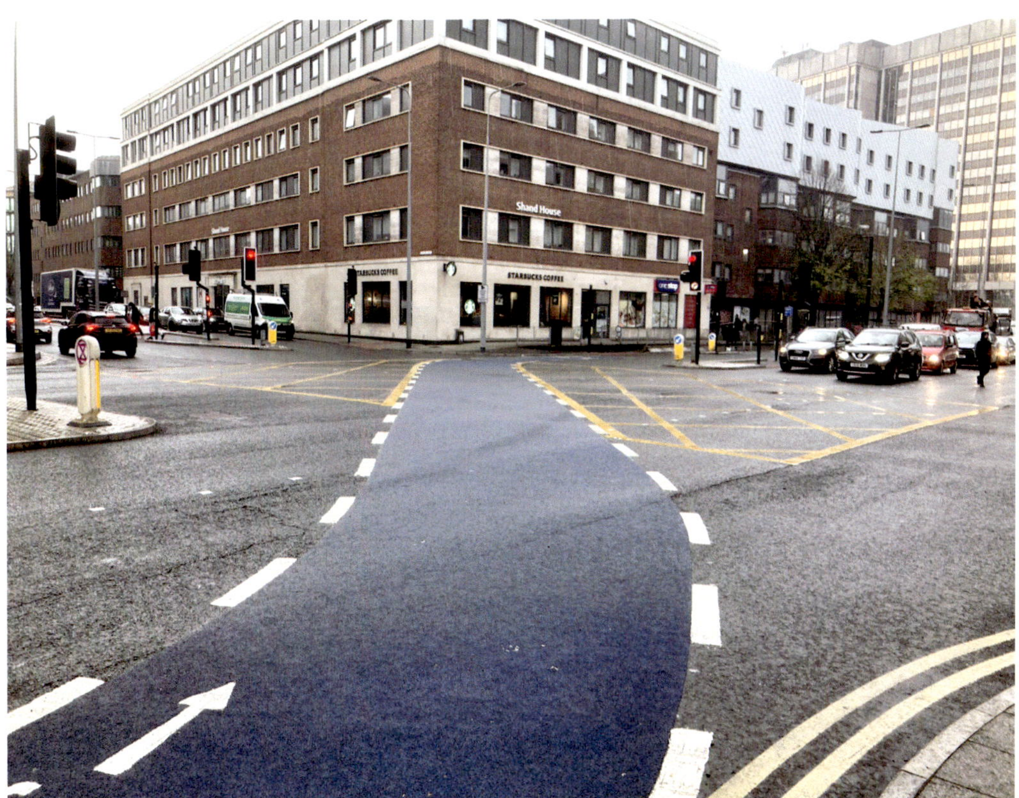

Shand House. (© Bibeyjj (Wikimedia, CC BY-SA 4.0))

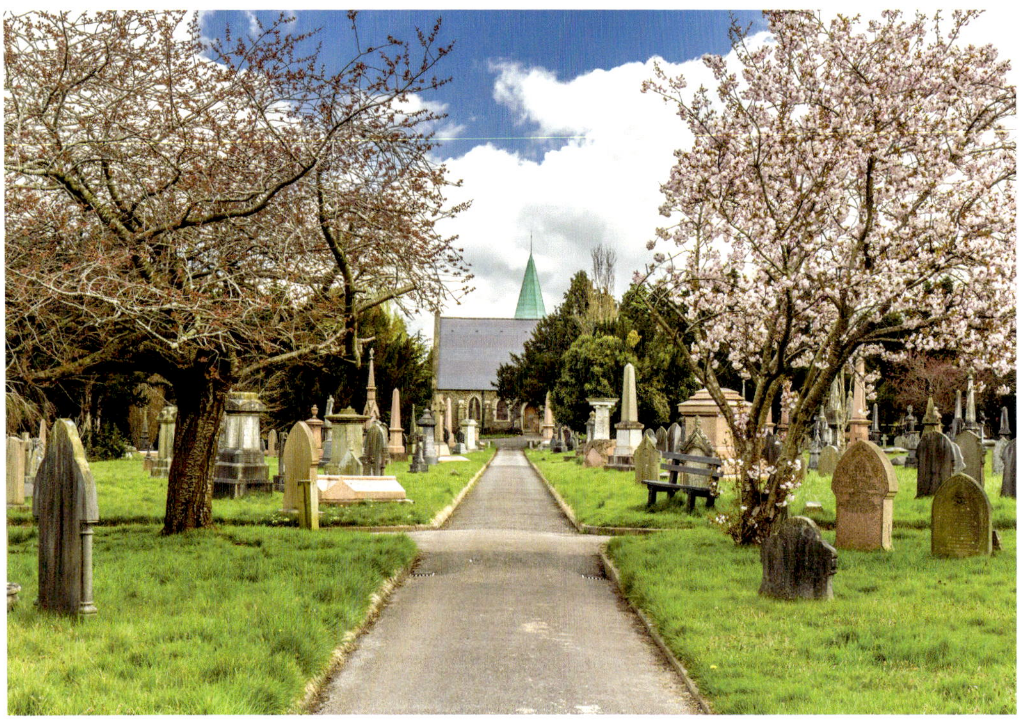

Cathays Cemetery. (© Robert Drózd (Flickr, CC BY-SA 2.0))

Motivated by a determined effort to alleviate the plight of the visually impaired, she established the Association for Improving the Social and Working Conditions of the Blind in 1865. From humble beginnings in a rented space in Canton, this organisation initially assisted a small number of people with pioneering initiatives that provided both employment and support. Her efforts eventually led to the establishment of the Cardiff Institute for the Blind, which has continued to help many people since then.

More than a century after the institution's founding, in 1984, the premises were renamed Shand House in tribute to her influence. Despite moving to Switzerland later in life, Shand's wish was to be buried back home in Wales, and she shares a grave and headstone with her brother in Cathays Cemetery.

Scars of History

To say Cardiff has been at the heart of Welsh history would be something of an understatement. From the arrival of the Romans to the Second World War, the now-bustling streets bear the marks of centuries gone by and, as such, are a treasure trove of historical wonders.

There's the newly resurrected dock feeder canal, for example, which stands as a testament to Cardiff's industrial power. And Dead Man's Alley, which conceals a macabre secret bang in the heart of town. But Cardiff's history isn't confined to grand monuments and solemn tombs. Beneath the mundane, archaeologists are continuously unearthing relics of a bygone era, from medieval buildings lurking under public conveniences to forgotten martyrs immortalised in bronze plaques.

In this chapter, we peel back the layers of time to uncover tales of triumph and tragedy that whisper the secrets of a city shaped by the passage of time.

The Hidden Canal
In 2023, one of Cardiff's hidden gems, concealed beneath the city for more than seventy years, began to re-emerge. Built nearly two centuries ago, the long-lost Churchill Way dock feeder canal offers a fascinating glimpse into Cardiff's

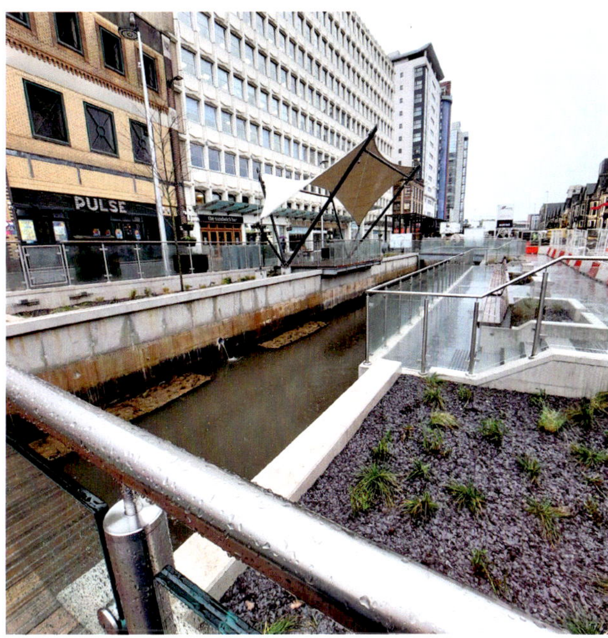

The canal on
Churchill Way.
(Photo by Emma Hardy)

industrial heritage. Having played a crucial role in the city's rise as a global business hub, it supported the transportation of coal and iron, which were vital to Cardiff's economic growth. However, it was covered up during the mid-twentieth century to make way for modern infrastructure.

Now, the dock feeder canal has been unveiled as the focal point of the city's Canal Quarter initiative, a regeneration project designed to manage traffic and enhance the urban landscape. The restoration involved removing massive concrete beams and introducing new features more suited to the modern world, such as rain gardens that purify surface water and divert it away from the sewage system. This project not only celebrates Cardiff's past but also incorporates sustainable urban development practices, blending history with innovation.

Dead Man's Alley

In the hustle and bustle of daily life, most people don't stop to consider what might be hidden beneath their feet as they navigate the crowded streets. Cardiff is a city criss-crossed with long-lost tunnels and concealed entrances hidden just below the surface, once serving all manner of purposes from the mundane to the macabre. One such alleyway can be found outside the city parish church of St John the Baptist in the city centre. It is marked with mysterious brass numbers on the paving stones, which relate to the path's rather ominous nickname: Dead Man's Alley.

The churchyard was once much larger, extending well beyond its current boundaries. When Cardiff Market opened in 1891, this proved to be something of a headache for marketgoers who, unable to walk directly through the churchyard to the market, were forced to take a lengthy detour up Working Street, past the church itself, around the bend, and back down again. It was agreed that, with the churchyard full to capacity, a pathway could be built across it to provide a shortcut to the market on Trinity Street. This would, however, mean that the public would be walking over the vaults below, and to ensure they could still be identified, numbers were placed on the paving stones to mark those buried beneath.

At the time, it was decided that the alley would remain the property of the church and, in a tradition that continues to this day, it was to be closed on Good Friday, the holy day on which Christians observe the crucifixion of Jesus. The council, in return, agreed to care for a part of the church now known as St John's Garden. The numbers on the stones have eroded with time, sometimes to the point where they can no longer be identified, but have been replaced more recently as close to their original positions as possible.

Another holy site with an eerie-sounding pathway running alongside it is Llandaff Cathedral. Adjacent to the extensively restored twelfth-century Gothic gem is Cathedral Close, a route dubbed 'the road of the dead'. According to tradition, it once led to a cemetery on the banks of the River Taff, and bodies would have been transported along it en route to their final resting place. In more recent times, sightings of ghostly children suggest that some may still haunt the area today, with paranormal investigators theorising that they might be victims of a nineteenth-century cholera outbreak.

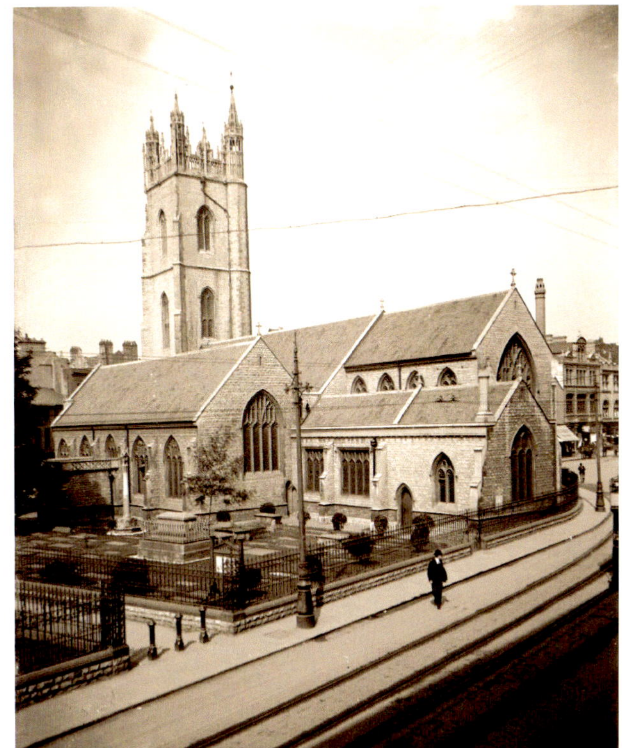

Right: St John the Baptist, *c.* 1905, with an entrance to 'Dead Man's Alley' on the left. (Martin Ridley photographic collection)

Below: The graveyard at St John the Baptist. (© Richard Williams (Flickr, CC BY-ND 4.0))

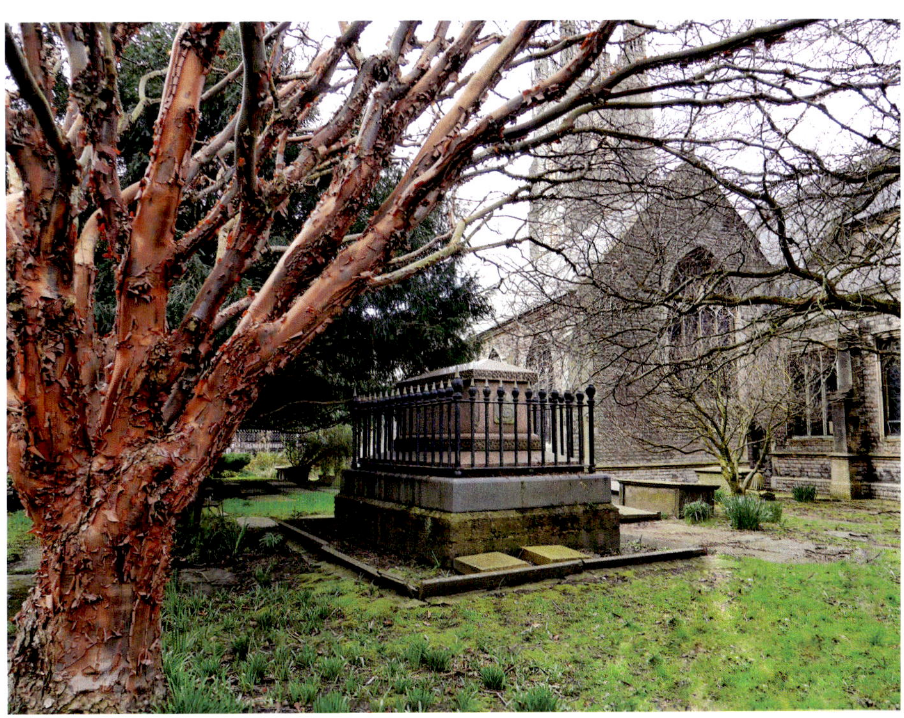

The Herbert Chapel Tomb

In the last entry, we explored Dead Man's Alley, a curiosity outside the city parish church of St John the Baptist. However, there are many more fascinating discoveries to be made inside. The Grade I listed church, described as 'the oldest building in the city centre', has been a continuous place of Christian worship for

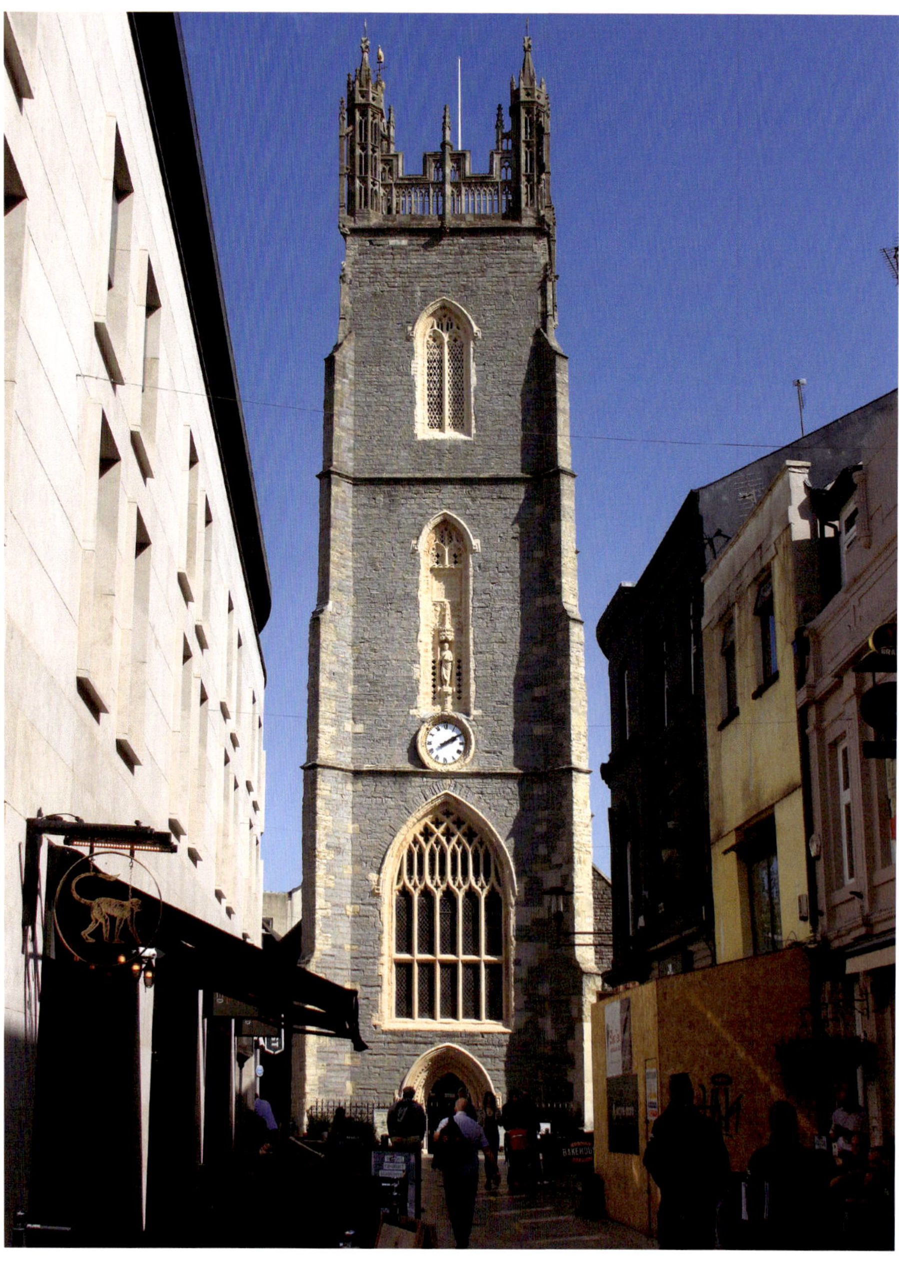

St John the Baptist. (© Ben Salter (Flickr, CC BY 4.0))

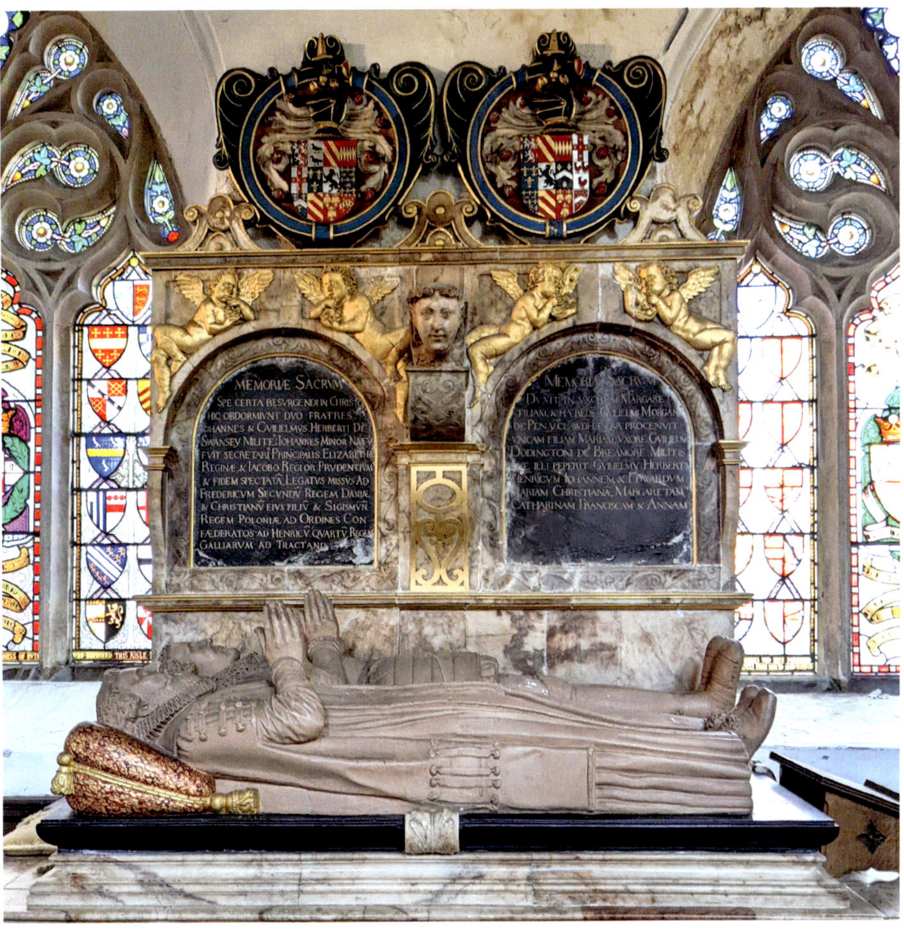

The Herbert tomb at St John the Baptist. (© The Wub (Wikimedia, CC BY-SA 4.0))

more than eight centuries. Built in the Perpendicular Gothic style, it is a significant reminder of Cardiff's medieval past.

A particular highlight is a grand tomb dedicated to two brothers who lie side by side in the Herbert Chapel. Besides being an excellent example of Jacobean art, the lives of the siblings it commemorates are equally interesting. One is Sir William Herbert, who died in 1609 and was the keeper of another surviving example of medieval Cardiff, Cardiff Castle. Beside him lies his multi-titled brother Sir John Herbert, whose extensive career includes stints as a lawyer, diplomat, and translator. He represented six constituencies in Parliament – including Gatton, Christchurch, Bodmin, and Monmouthshire and Glamorgan in Wales – and served as Secretary of State under both Elizabeth I and James I, as well as a distinguished ambassador in Denmark and Poland, undertaking important diplomatic missions. He was appointed High Sheriff of Glamorgan in 1605 and passed away in 1617, just two months after fighting a duel with Sir Lewis Tresham.

Other points of interest include the shimmering stained-glass windows behind the tomb that display the coats of arms of families connected to Cardiff Castle; a Renaissance screen surrounding the Herbert Chapel, on which are carved two faces that reference a legend relating to the crucifixion of Jesus; the south chancel aisle, the oldest part of the church where the Grade I listed organ is located; and its 130-foot tower, on the west side of which is an effigy of the patron saint beneath a tablet dating the tower to 1473.

The Hidden Medieval Building

In 2019, archaeologists had quite a surprise during a community dig on the site of former public toilets in Llandaff. Situated next to the Bishop's Palace, a Grade I listed building dating from the thirteenth century, they hoped to uncover something of interest. However, they likely did not expect to discover something as significant as a medieval building, which, due to its prominent location in such a historic part of town, is believed to have belonged to a person of considerable importance.

The ruins of the Bishop's Palace, a short walk from Llandaff Cathedral, are all that remain of the bishop's residence in the town. It is believed that the buildings were originally damaged and abandoned following an attack by Owain Glyndŵr during his rebellion against the Kingdom of England in the early 1400s. The clergy fled the assault and did not return for several centuries, only re-establishing their presence in the Victorian era.

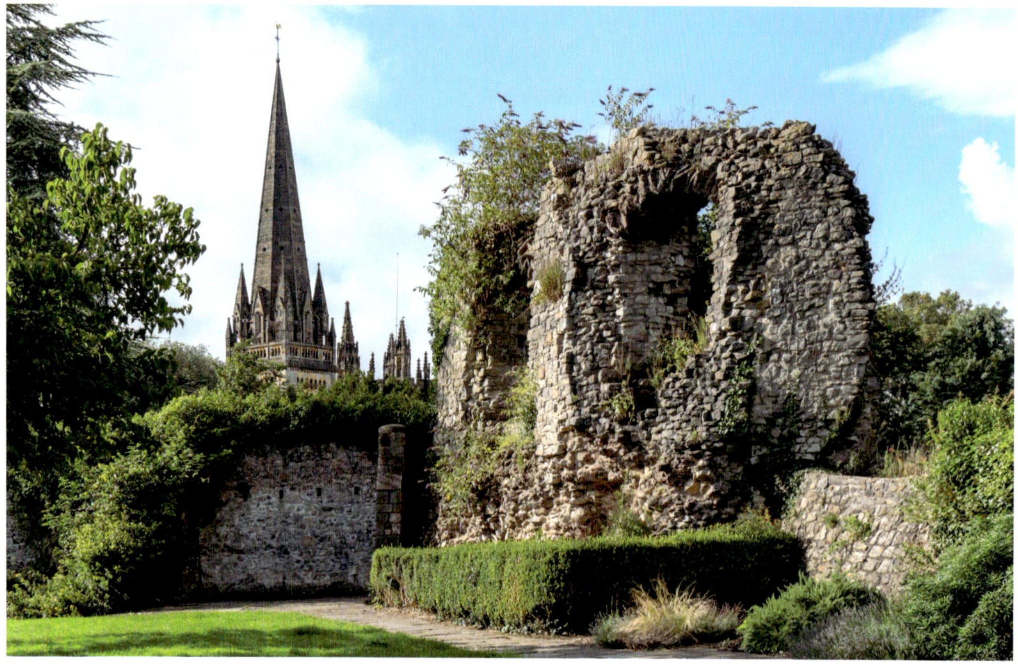

The ruins of the Old Bishop's Palace with the spire of Llandaff Cathedral in the background. (© Dominic Nelson (Wikimedia, CC BY-SA 4.0 DEED))

The public toilets, on the other hand, were a far more recent addition. Dating from the 1930s, they also occupied a site with a fascinating history, an area known as 'the pound' since the 1600s where animals were kept. The house discovered below, measuring roughly 10 metres in length, was dated to around 1450. The use of Bath stone in the fireplace, a luxury item at the time, suggests the owner was a person of some standing. Other items of note include chequered floor tiles, an early fourteenth-century jeton (a coin-like token thought to have originated in Paris), and, harking back to its time as 'the pound', the remains of animals.

After the discovery, the site was covered over once more to allow for the construction of a new community and heritage centre. While the medieval building may not be visible, anyone who visits will know they are standing on a piece of history.

The Secret Church

One of Cardiff's best-loved quirky attractions is the so-called 'secret church' that, for a long time, was tucked away inside a major shopping retailer on St Mary Street.

Bethany Particular Baptist Chapel was originally built in 1807 and underwent several extensions and rebuilds throughout the nineteenth century. It was no small place of worship; it could accommodate up to 950 parishioners, complete with a Sunday school and burial ground. The front featured arched windows

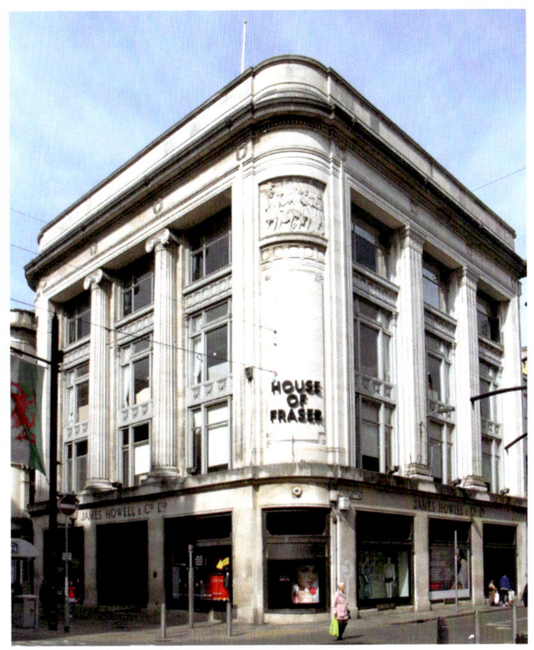

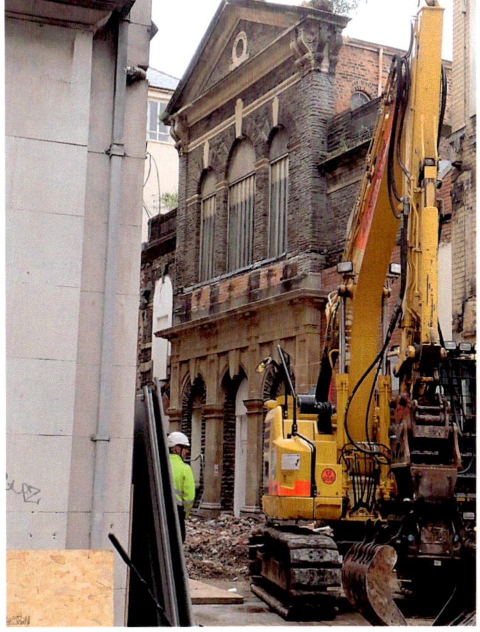

Above left: The House of Fraser building as it was in 2015. (© Tony Hisgett (Flickr, CC BY 4.0))

Above right: Bethany Baptist Chapel is revealed during building work in 2023. (© Rhyswynne (Wikimedia, CC BY-SA 4.0))

decorated with stained glass, while arcades of similar windows lined its sides. A domed belfry rose from the centre of the roof.

Its prime location in Cardiff's main commercial district meant that surrounding buildings expanded over time, and by the 1960s, the congregation had relocated to Rhiwbina. The chapel became part of the growing Howells department store, now a Grade II* listed building that first opened its doors in 1867. Rather than demolish the chapel, it was incorporated into the store itself. Several original features, such as the front arches and cast-iron pillars, remained visible to shoppers and were retained when the building was bought by House of Fraser in 1972.

The department store closed its doors to customers for the last time in 2023 and was acquired by the Thackeray Group, who soon began renovations to transform the building into a multifunctional space including residential flats. During these renovations, the church, remarkably preserved within the store, became visible once more from the street. Also revealed to the public was a unique memorial, which will be explored in our next entry.

The Forgotten Martyr

A memorial plaque commemorating a martyr who was burned at the stake in the sixteenth century can be found in a recess to the right of the front door of Bethany Particular Baptist Chapel on St Mary Street and was, for a long time, only visible

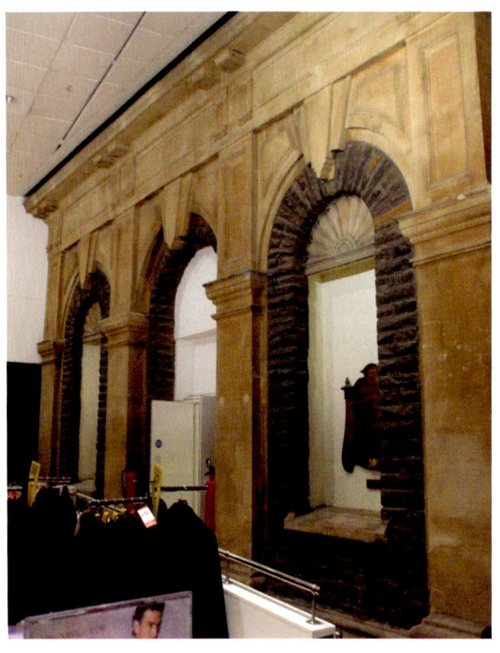

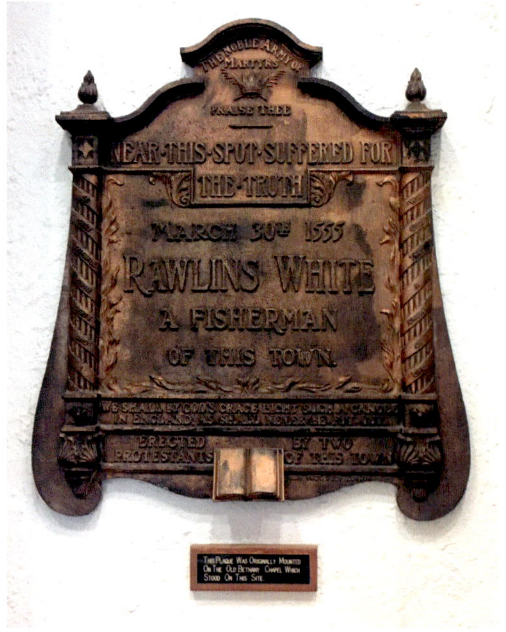

Above left: The entrance to Bethany Baptist Church within the store. (© John Lord (Wikimedia, CC BY-SA 4.0 DEED))

Above right: Rawlins White's memorial plaque. (© Ham II (Wikimedia, CC BY-SA 4.0))

inside a department store. The plaque reads: 'The Noble Army of Martyrs praise thee / Near this spot / March 30th 1555 / Rawlins White / A fisherman of this town.'

Rawlins White, as the plaque suggests, was indeed a local fisherman, but much more besides – and it was not the fishing that led to his martyrdom. During the reign of Mary I, who reinstated Roman Catholicism, openly professing Protestant beliefs became perilous. Despite being illiterate, White learned the Bible from his son and became a respected preacher and local leader, leading to conflict with the bishop of Llandaff. Imprisoned for his beliefs, White faced horrendous conditions and a gruesome death. Nevertheless, he remained steadfast and even jovial as he awaited his punishment, supposedly declining all opportunities to recant.

White was eventually led to the stake and burned. While doubts persist regarding the exact date and location of his execution, it is certain that this Cardiff man paid the ultimate price for his convictions under the rule of the queen dubbed 'Bloody Mary'. Just three years later, her half-sister Elizabeth I ascended to the throne and reversed such policies.

The Cathedral's Revolutionary Art

Llandaff Cathedral stands as a testament to centuries of Christian worship and architectural evolution in Wales. Dating back to the sixth century, the cathedral, as we see it today, is primarily of Norman origin with Gothic ornamentation.

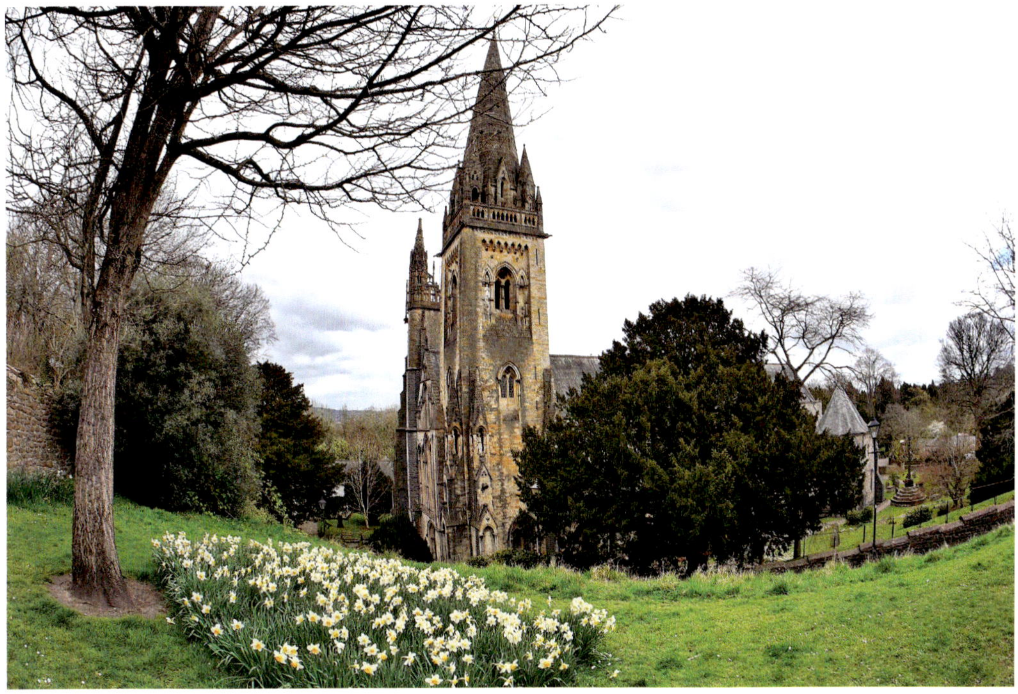

Llandaff Cathedral. (© Richard Williams (Flickr, CC BY-ND 2.0))

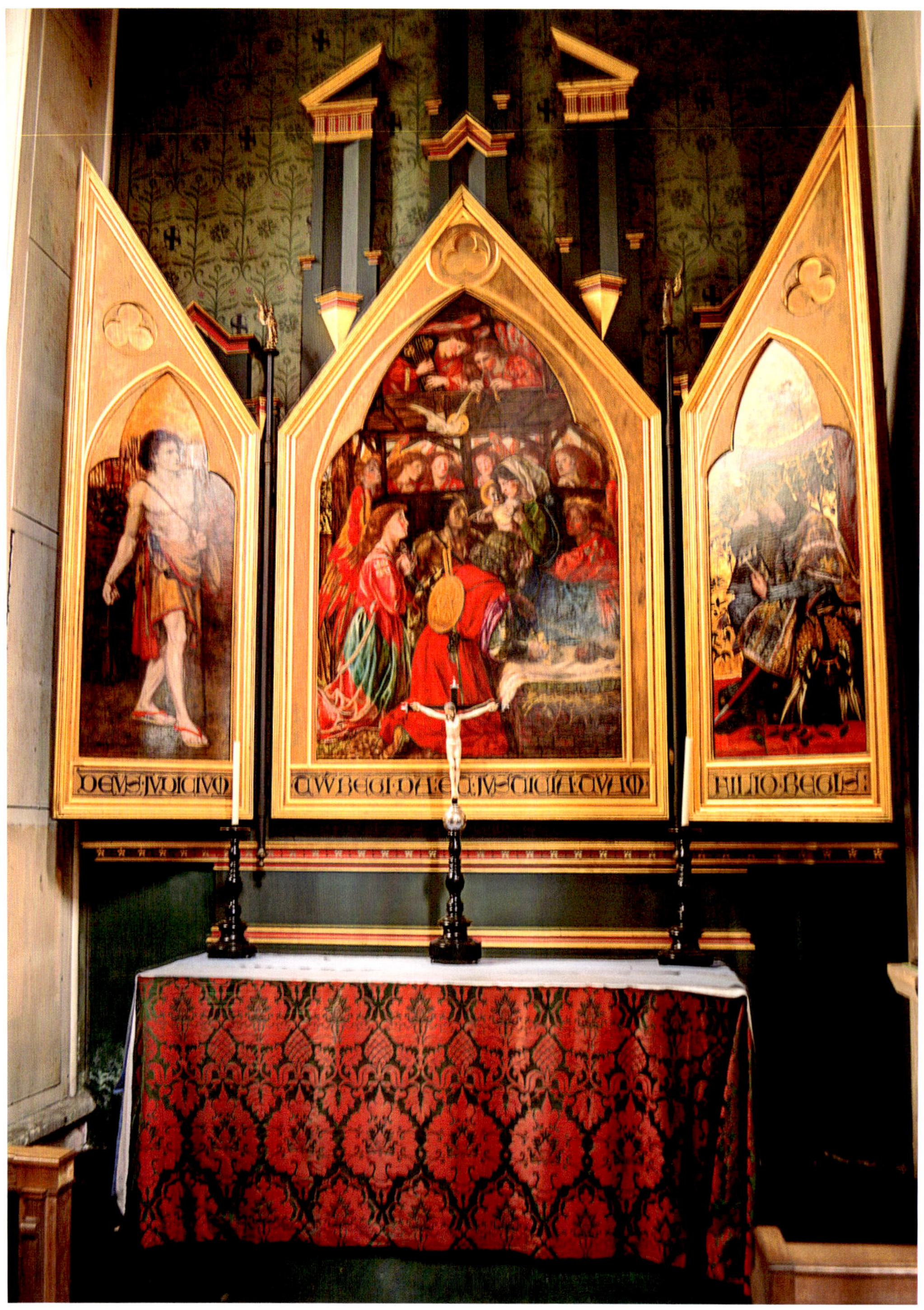

The Rossetti Triptych. (© Andrew Rees (Flickr, CC BY-ND 2.0))

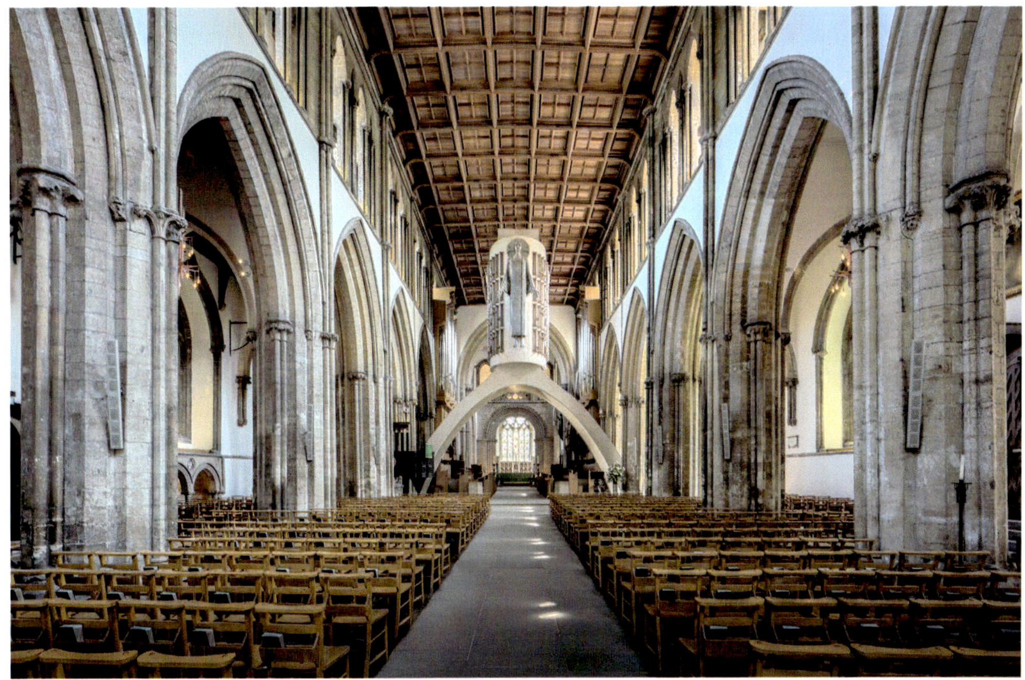

'Christ in Glory' at Llandaff Cathedral. (© Michael D Beckwith (Flickr, CC0 1.0))

It has witnessed significant upheavals and restorations over the years, from Owain Glyndŵr's rebellion in the early 1400s and the Great Storm of 1703 to the eighteenth-century collapse of the south-east tower and the wartime devastation during the Second World War.

The cathedral's evolution extends beyond architecture. Its history is interwoven with remarkable, centuries-spanning works of art, each enriching the spiritual and cultural tapestry of the building and warranting further exploration. One notable example is the Bishop Marshall Panel, a late medieval painting depicting the Assumption of the Virgin Mary into heaven. This poignant artwork, created on Welsh oak, was once part of the episcopal throne of John Marshall, Bishop of Llandaff, in the late fifteenth century. As the sole surviving piece from the throne, it has been restored and conserved and was placed in its current position in 2021.

Unusually for a cathedral, Llandaff has occasionally found itself at the cutting edge of the art world, even courting controversy by commissioning contemporary artists. Such decisions, though contentious at the time, have proven to be shrewd in the long term. One notable example is the Rossetti Triptych in the Illtyd Chapel. Commissioned from Pre-Raphaelite leader Dante Gabriel Rossetti by the dean and chapter in 1855, the triptych was designed for the Illtyd Chapel and took nearly a decade to realise, finally arriving in 1864. With its vivid colours and medieval-inspired iconography, it embodies the Brotherhood's bohemian ethos and outright defiance of Royal Academy conventions and Mannerist traditions.

Offering an unconventional take on the Nativity, Rossetti's symbolic representation emphasises Christ's lineage from both wealth and poverty, with a poor shepherd boy on the left and a wealthy king on the right. In the centre, the Nativity scene shows the Christ child favouring the shepherd over the king, offering one his hand and the other his foot, suggesting the supremacy of the poor over the rich. The scene is populated with figures modelled on real people, including fellow Pre-Raphaelites like William Morris and Edward Burne-Jones.

In the mid-twentieth century, George Pace, architect to the dean and chapter of Llandaff Cathedral, noted the absence of a medieval pulpitum – a screen that traditionally divides the choir from the nave and ambulatory – making the cathedral resemble a large parish church. He proposed constructing an arch to support part of the organ and display contemporary art without obstructing ground-level views. The winning design featured a double wishbone concrete arch housing part of the organ and a figure of 'Christ in Majesty' by Jacob Epstein. Like Rossetti, Epstein was a contentious choice, and an alternative suggestion was a more traditional painting by Stanley Spencer. Despite this, the War Damage Commission funded the aluminium casting, and now the towering Christ figure, which gazes through the west window to the world beyond, has become synonymous with the cathedral and is a remarkable example of the power of modern religious art.

The Magical Roof Garden

If there's one place in Cardiff that truly encapsulates the personality and eccentricities of its owner, it's the roof garden in Cardiff Castle. An exclusive space created for Lord Bute's personal contemplation, it draws inspiration from biblical miracles to ancient Rome, with visits to Pompeii, his devout faith, and a fascination with all things medieval revealing themselves in the design.

Located at the tip of Bute Tower, the garden was designed by William Burges and constructed between 1873 and 1876. Burges, a close confidante of John Crichton-Stuart, 3rd Marquess of Bute, also designed Castell Coch and shared Bute's passion for Catholicism and medievalism. The garden is Roman in style, inspired by villas they admired in Pompeii. The mosaic floor is bordered with pink Peterhead granite, a nod to Bute's Scottish heritage. The tiled walls illustrate stories of the prophet Elijah from the Old Testament, with Hebrew inscriptions reflecting Bute's scholarly interest.

The garden's most prominent feature is the bronze Madonna and child by Italian sculptor Ceccardo Egidio Fucigna, who also created the statue of the Virgin watching over Castell Coch's doorway. At its centre sits a bronze fountain featuring beavers holding fish, the mouths of which act as water spouts. Other animal-inspired features include a stag's head statue, camel paintings and bronze flower boxes copied from Roman charcoal burners excavated at Pompeii.

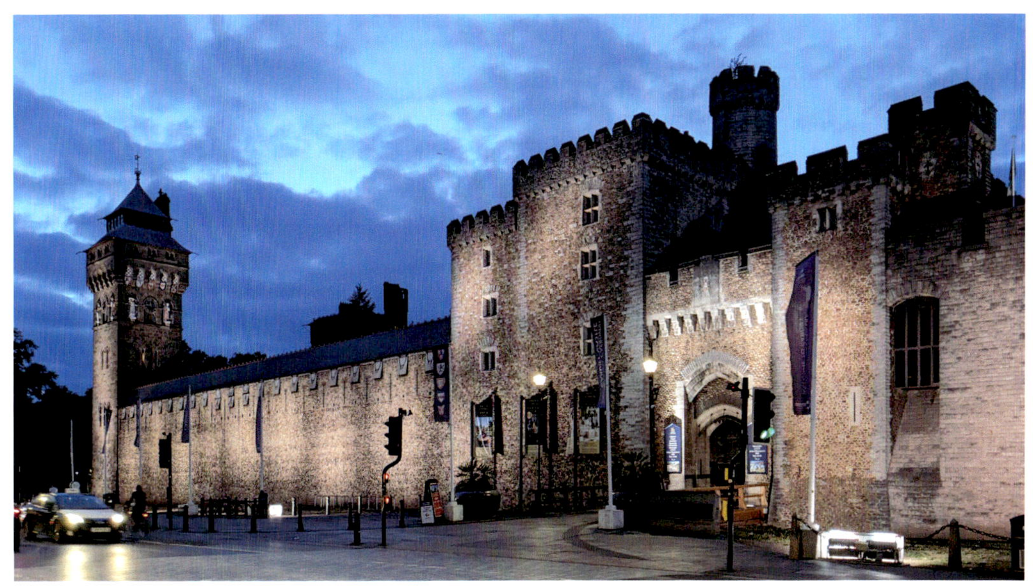

Cardiff Castle south gate and clock tower. (© The wub (Wikimedia, CC BY-SA 4.0))

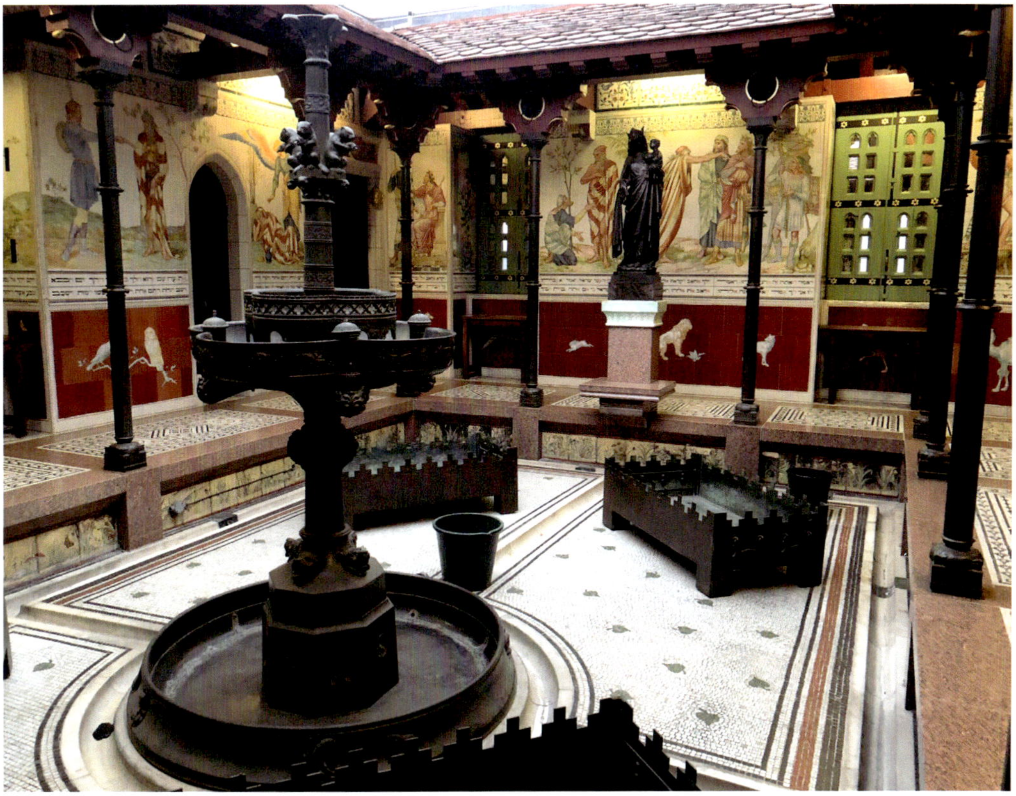

The Roof Garden at Cardiff Castle. (© KJP1 (Wikimedia, CC BY-SA 4.0))

Famous Faces

Cardiff's most important feature is its people. While some achieve superstardom, you don't need to be Gareth Bale to be ranked among the great Cardiffians who make a difference to their hometown each and every day. From adventurers to activists, performers to politicians, the Welsh capital has long been home to an eclectic mix of personalities who have forged its history and enriched its heritage.

But it's not only long-term residents that have left an indelible mark. Even a fleeting visit can have an impact that reverberates through the centuries, such as the legacy of Captain Scott's lavish farewell feast, or the captivating performances of Buffalo Bill's Wild West show. Mahatma Gandhi never even set foot in the city, and yet his statue in Cardiff Bay serves as an inspiration to many.

In this chapter, we'll take a closer look at some of the faces that reflect the diversity and dynamism of Cardiff, exploring places linked to their tales of triumph and tragedy, resilience and determination.

The Captain Scott Room

On 15 June 1910, the *Terra Nova* – a converted whaler – set sail from Cardiff on an ill-fated expedition to the South Pole. Two days earlier, Captain Robert Falcon Scott and his crew had enjoyed an eye-wateringly large farewell feast in the city, which consisted of thirteen courses, including Baked Alaska for dessert. Tragically, the expedition would not end as hoped; it was a voyage from which the much-celebrated captain would not return, and his men were beaten to the South Pole by a Norwegian team led by Roald Amundsen, who reached the pole on 14 December 1911.

Hosted by the Cardiff Chamber of Commerce, the grand Alexandra Room in the Royal Hotel on St Mary Street was prepared for the occasion. This space, now a meticulously preserved Grade II listed room with rich mahogany panelling, has been renamed the Captain Scott Room in his honour. Preserved artefacts from the dinner offer a fascinating glimpse into their entertainment that night, with the programme of music discovered in 1982 revealing that Robert's Band performed a selection of operatic tunes from the likes of Verdi and Gounod, before sending them on their way with Blankenburg's *Farewell to Gladiators* and a toast to the king and all those sailing on the *Terra Nova*.

But that's not the only interesting fact about 'Cardiff's oldest surviving hotel'. With a history spanning more than 150 years, it originally housed some seventy rooms, with the boom in industry at the turn of the twentieth century leading to some lavish additions and renovations, from staff accommodation to a regal staircase. It's also not the only memorial to Scott to be found in the city. Along

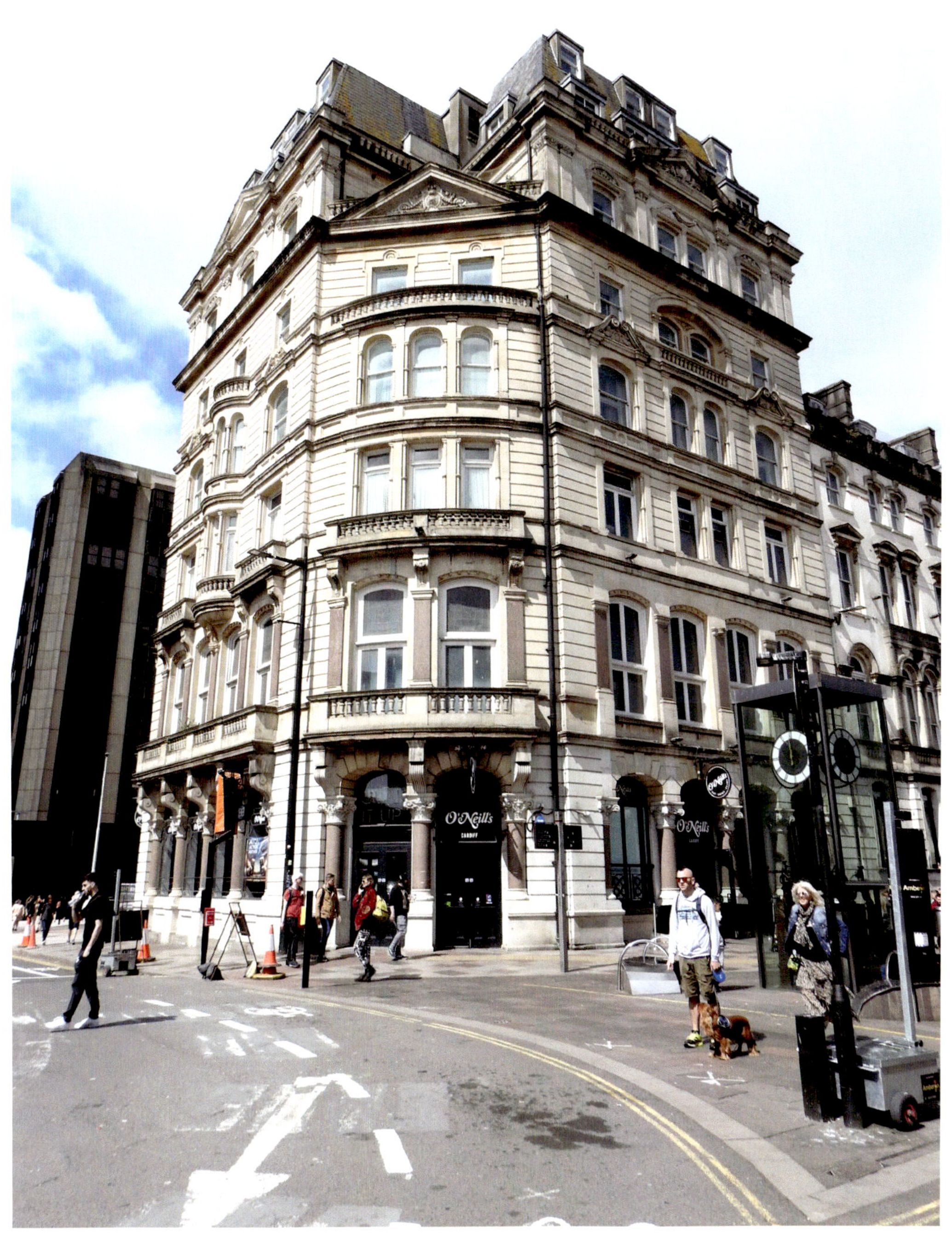

The Royal Hotel. (© Reading Tom (Flickr, CC BY 2.0))

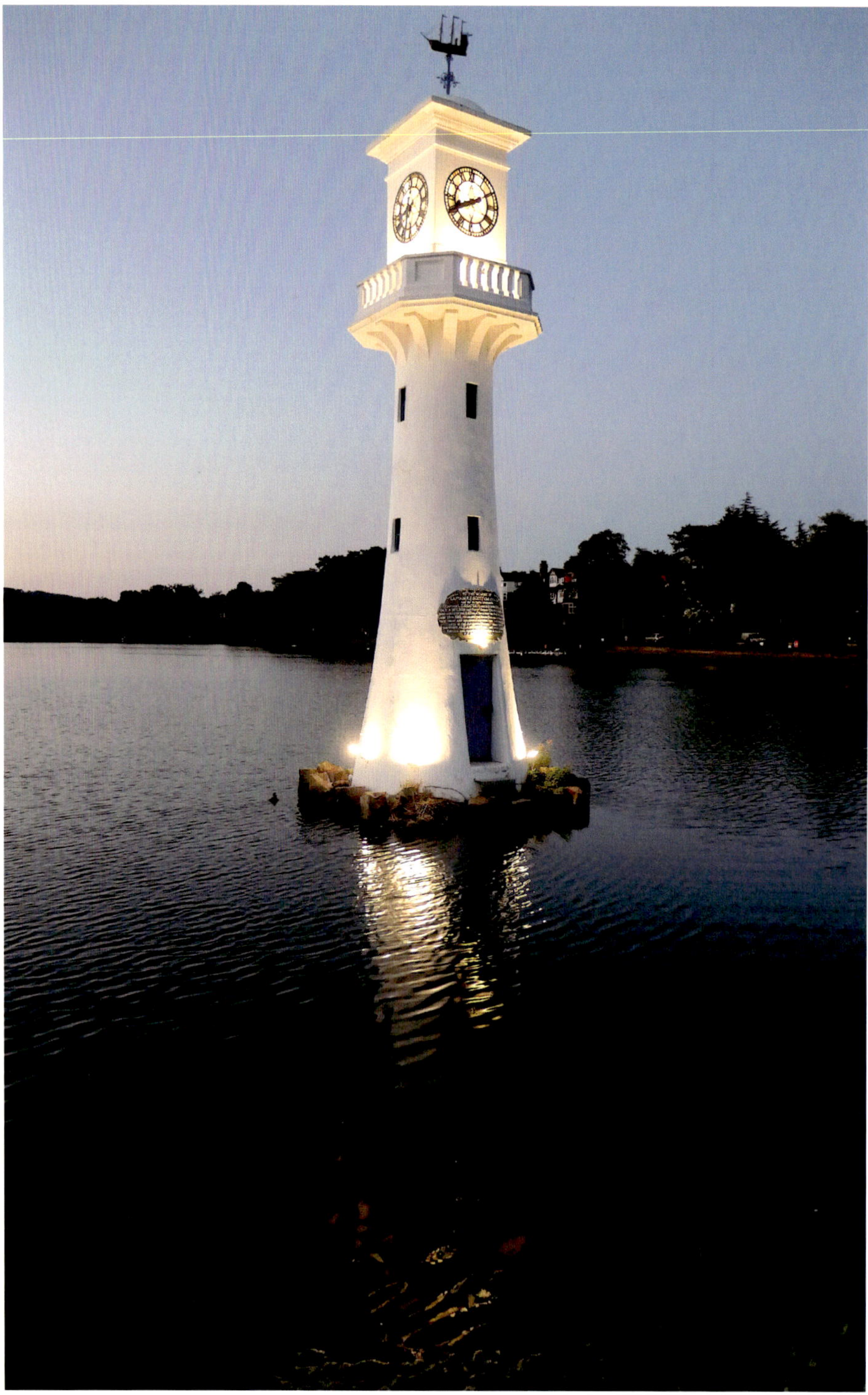

Captain Scott Memorial in Roath Park. (© Richard Szwejkowski (Flickr, CC BY-SA 2.0))

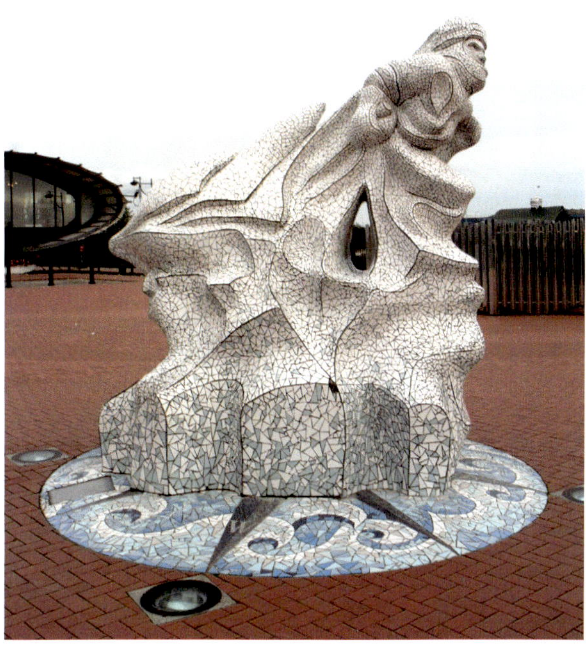

Captain Scott Memorial in
Cardiff Bay. (© Tony Hisgett
(Flickr, CC BY 2.0))

with the Coal Exchange mentioned in the first chapter, an impressive memorial sculpture of Scott himself battling against the elements was unveiled in Cardiff Bay by HRH The Princess Royal on 6 June 2003.

An earlier memorial in the shape of a lighthouse, known locally as the 'Clock Tower', can be found lighting the waters of the lake in Roath Park, which was drained for its installation. Dating from 1914, a plaque on its side reads: 'To the memory of Captain R. F. Scott C.V.O., D.S.O., R.N. and his faithful companions Captain L.E.G. Oates, Lieut. H.R. Bowers R.I.M., Dr. E.A. Wilson and Petty Officer Edgar Evans R.N. who sailed in the S.S. Terra Nova from the Port of Cardiff June 15th 1910, to locate the South Pole; and, in pursuit of that great and successful scientific task, laid down their lives in the Antarctic Regions. March 1912. "Britons all, and very gallant gentlemen". Erected and presented to the City of Cardiff by F.C. Bowring Esq., J.P. 1915.'

Mahatma Gandhi Statue

On 2 October 2017, the 148th anniversary of the birth of Mahatma Gandhi was celebrated in Cardiff with the unveiling of an impressive 6-foot tribute. Holding a staff in one hand and the Bhagavad Gita (Hindu scripture) in the other, a bronze statue of the revered Indian leader was revealed at the end of Lloyd George Avenue in Cardiff Bay in the presence of dignitaries, including Gandhi's grandson. The £65,000 work of public art was paid for by donations to the Hindu Council of Wales and created by the Indian father-and-son team of Ram and Anil Sutar.

The ceremony coincided with the 70th anniversary of India's independence, during which Gandhi found global recognition for his non-violent resistance and

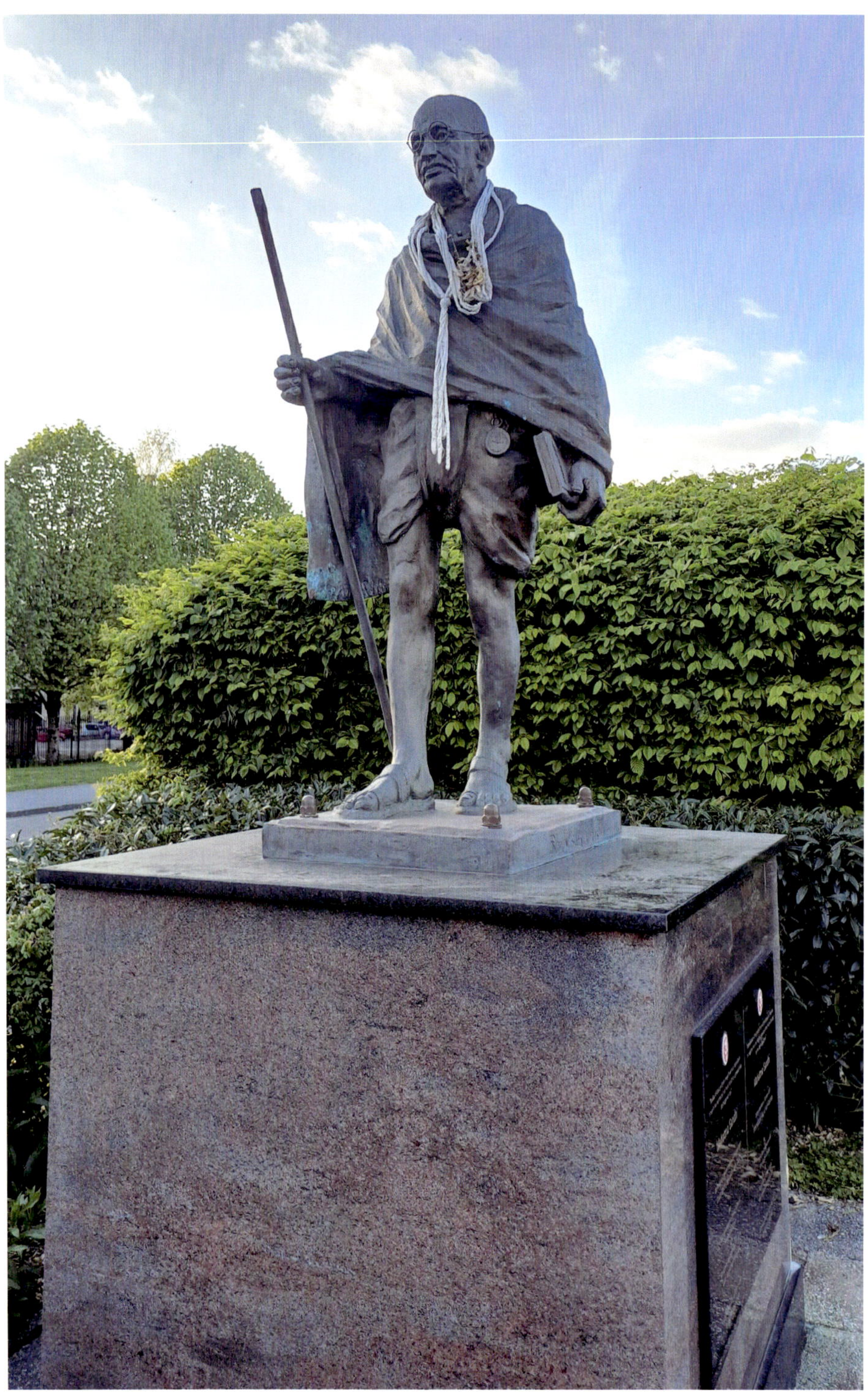

Mahatma Gandhi statue in Cardiff Bay.

his advocacy of tolerance. The statue also symbolises the cultural and trade ties between India and Wales and shines a light on an overlooked historical connection between Gandhi and former Prime Minister David Lloyd George, whose advocacy for the Welsh language inspired Gandhi's commitment to preserving language.

Buffalo Bill Rides In

Born in 1846, Buffalo Bill – aka William Frederick Cody – was a legendary figure of the American Wild West. He captivated audiences across the United States and further afield in the late nineteenth and early twentieth centuries with his larger-than-life persona and thrilling performances. That was certainly the case on his visits to Cardiff, having been persuaded to visit Wales by opera superstar Adelina Patti.

Bill lived a life filled with adventure, serving as a soldier, buffalo hunter, and gold prospector among other occupations. He gained widespread fame as a showman, particularly through his traveling spectacle, Buffalo Bill's Wild West Show. Featuring a colourful cast of performers, the show included sharpshooters and re-enactments of frontier life, which showcased the rugged essence of the American West to audiences far and wide. Despite controversies regarding the portrayal of Native Americans and a romanticisation of the Wild West, Bill's legacy endures as a powerful symbol of American culture.

He first visited the Welsh capital in 1891, accompanied by an impressive entourage that included 200 horses and eighteen buffalo. By the end of his fourth and final show in Sophia Gardens, in which he was joined by sharpshooter Annie Oakley, it was reported that an astonishing 126,400 people had witnessed the spectacle. Cardiff became an important stop on his European tours, continuously drawing large crowds who flocked to watch his daring feats and thrilling performances. From stagecoach robberies to expert displays of marksmanship, these shows offered a glimpse into a world vastly different from Wales's industrial

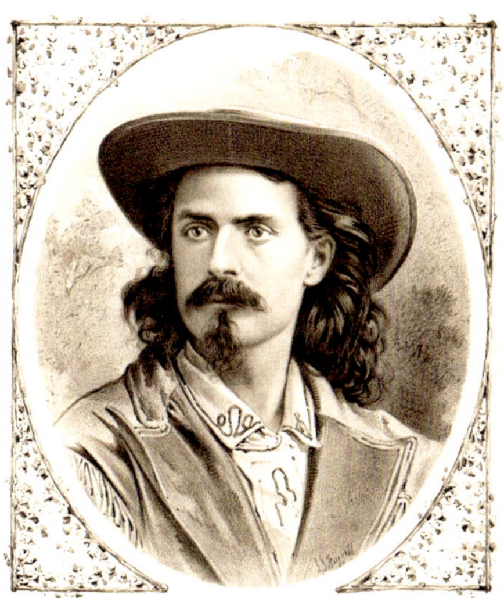

Portrait of Buffalo Bill.

landscape, leaving a lasting impression on the local community. They offered a form of escapism and entertainment for audiences of all ages, sparking a curiosity about the American frontier and its iconic figures. Bill's final show in the city took place in 1904.

Roald Dahl's Family Roots

It's no secret that Roald Dahl, the author of such children's favourites as *Charlie and the Chocolate Factory* (1964), *The BFG* (1982) and *Matilda* (1988) – not to mention his adult works – was born in Llandaff, Cardiff, on 13 September 1916. But beyond the well-known stories, the city itself holds lesser-known connections to his early life and inspirations.

Today, the streets that sparked his imagination can still be explored, while Roald Dahl Plass, a significant public space named in his honour, is the home of Wales's twin institutions of government and culture: the Senedd and Wales Millennium Centre. There are also more subtle signs of his time in the area, such as the sculpture of a crocodile lurking in Cardiff Bay.

In September 2016, Cardiff celebrated Dahl's centenary with the Roald Dahl 100 Weekend, a suitably over-the-top party that saw the streets packed with fans from around the world. Activities, performances, workshops, and exhibitions ran from dawn until late into the night, with a highlight being the sight of a giant peach being paraded through the streets.

Despite Dahl's eventual move away from Wales, settling in Great Missenden, Buckinghamshire, in 1954 where he is buried, his roots in Cardiff remained strong. The Norwegian Church in Cardiff Bay holds particular significance, as

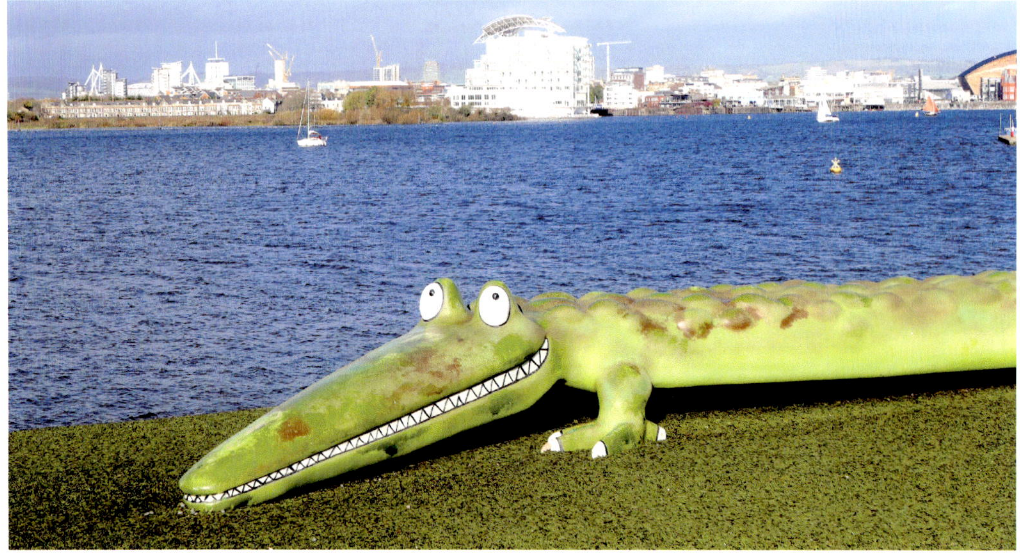

The Enormous Crocodile statue in Cardiff Bay during the Roald Dahl 100 Weekend celebration in 2020. (© Richard Szwejkowski (Flickr, CC BY-SA 2.0))

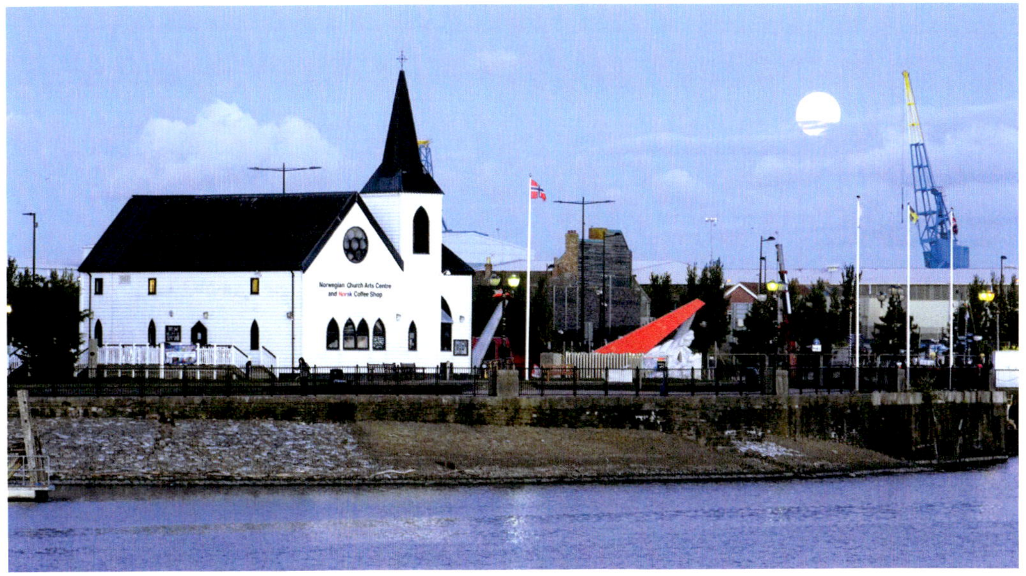

The Norwegian Church in Cardiff Bay. (© Chris Sampson (Flickr, CC BY-SA 2.0))

it was where Dahl was baptised and visited with his family. This church was a focal point for Cardiff's Norwegian community who, like Dahl's Oslo-born father Harald, were drawn to the docks by the industry. Harald established his shipbroking business in a room on Bute Street and built the family home Villa Marie, later known as Tŷ Gwyn, on Fairwater Road, where Dahl was born in 1916.

The family moved briefly to Tŷ-Mynydd in nearby Radyr in 1917, and when Harald died, he was buried in St John's Church. His mother, Sofie Magdalene, returned to Llandaff with the children in 1921, living in Cumberland Lodge, which is now Howell's School nursery. She was also buried in St John's, as was Dahl's elder half-sister Astri, in the family plot that is marked by a Celtic cross.

Shirley Bassey's Old Haunts

There are several places across Cardiff associated with Dame Shirley Bassey, the iconic chart-topper born on 8 January 1937 in Tiger Bay. The memorial to her birthplace, however, is not a statue or a blue plaque, but something more subtle; in fact, blink and you'll miss it.

Bassey, who made history as the first Welsh singer to reach number one on the singles chart in 1959 with 'As I Love You', rose to international fame with her powerful and soulful vocals. With a remarkable career that has spanned more than six decades, she became a cultural icon both at home and abroad, particularly known for her iconic James Bond theme songs 'Goldfinger' and 'Diamonds are Forever'.

The youngest of six children, who also lived with two half-sisters, Bassey was born at No. 182 Bute Street above the former Canadian Café on the main road

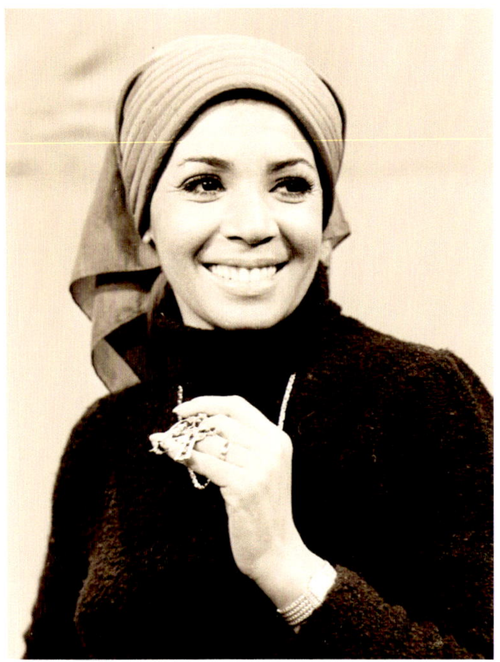
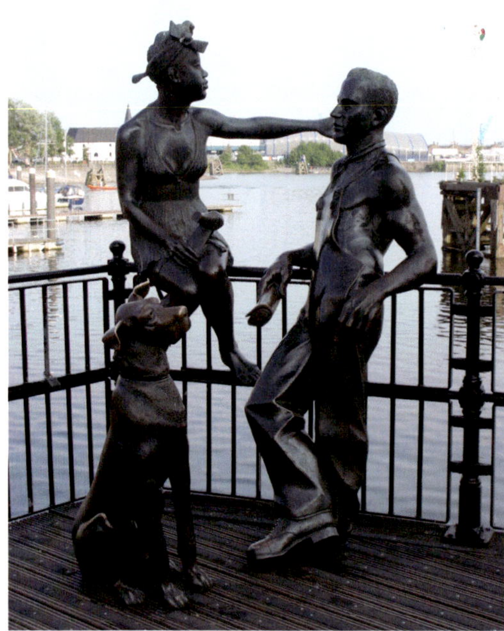

Above left: Shirley Bassey in 1971. (Wikimedia, CC0 1.0)

Above right: The *People Like Us* sculpture that commemorates the culture of Tiger Bay in modern-day Cardiff Bay. (© Richard Sutcliffe (Wikimedia, CC BY-SA 2.0))

in Tiger Bay. While her birthplace is no longer standing, it has been marked by a stone marker in the pavement, a plain square with her name in a circle.

Bassey wasn't in Tiger Bay for long; her family moved to nearby Splott when she was two years old. Anyone looking to walk in her footsteps there can stroll along Portmanmoor Road where her childhood home once stood. At the time there was a steelworks nearby that provided employment opportunities for many, along with a number of pubs such as the Bomb and Dagger and the Lord Wimborne, where she began singing. Although the area has since transformed beyond recognition with no remaining houses or pubs, nearby places such as Moorland Primary School, where she was encouraged to sing as a child, and the refurbished New Fleurs Social Club, where she sang when a little older, still bear connections to her early years. Additionally, the New Theatre in the city is where a seventeen-year-old Bassey made her professional debut in 'Hot From Harlem'.

Benjamin Disraeli's Bust

There's a historic building in Cardiff with quite a big claim to fame; not only was it one of Cardiff's oldest pubs, but it is also where Benjamin Disraeli, the Earl of Beaconsfield, supposedly spent the night on a visit to the city.

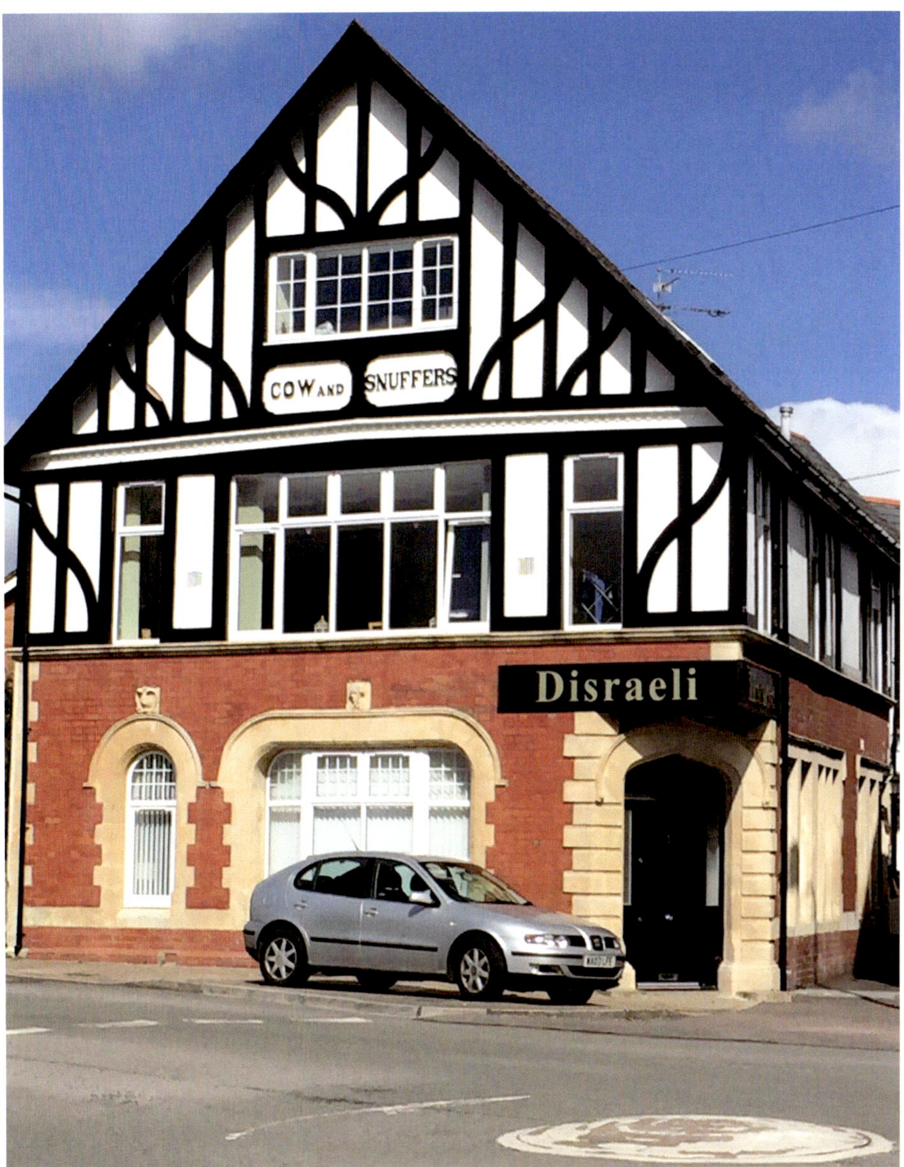

The Cow and Snuffers/Disraeli House. (© Alan Hughes (Wikimedia, CC BY-SA 2.0))

A politician, novelist and bon viveur, Disraeli – the first British Prime Minister of Jewish birth – held office twice: briefly in 1868 and again from 1874 to 1880. Nicknamed Dizzy, an endearing moniker related to his quick wit and sharp thinking, he struck up a close relationship with reigning monarch Queen Victoria, and was actively involved in politics until the year he died in 1881.

Tradition holds that Disraeli stayed overnight and enjoyed a drink at the Cow and Snuffers in Llandaff North. This uniquely named nineteenth-century inn, built in the Tudor style as a coach house, is thought to have been constructed to service the nearby Glamorganshire Canal. Having called last orders in 2010, it has since been transformed into flats, but evidence of Disraeli's supposed time there is commemorated in a work of art: a bust of the man himself above the door. Gone but not forgotten, it would be decorated with primroses on the anniversary of his death every 19 April.

While there might be doubt as to where exactly Disraeli stayed in the city, he certainly visited Cardiff and found more than a drink and a bed for the night. Disraeli was in the area in 1838 following the death of Cardiff MP Wyndham Lewis, who had financed his election, and became better acquainted with his widow, Mary. Eighteen months later, they were married.

In a totally unrelated tale, the pub has also entered the realm of folklore as a location visited by the Gwrach y Rhibyn, a witch-like figure known as the 'hag of the mist' in English. This terrifying death omen, which shares some similarities with the Irish banshee, was seen entering the premises late one evening. According to the story, one of the inmates died soon afterwards.

The Betty Campbell Monument

On 29 September 2021, a sculpture commemorating Wales's first black head teacher was unveiled by Monumental Welsh Women on the streets of Cardiff. Betty Campbell, born Rachel Elizabeth Johnson in Butetown in 1934, was a pioneering educator and community activist, known for her resilience and determination. The daughter of a Welsh Barbadian mother and a Jamaican father who died young in the Second World War, she excelled academically and, despite having the odds stacked against her, rose to the top position at Mount Stuart Primary School.

Campbell's career was characterised by innovation and advocacy, implementing groundbreaking educational approaches and actively promoting multiculturalism and social justice. Inspired by the civil rights movement in America, she integrated lessons on slavery, black history, and apartheid into the school curriculum, challenging norms and fostering understanding among her students. Beyond her role in education, Campbell's impact extended to community activism and political engagement, serving as an independent councillor for Butetown on Cardiff Council. She received numerous accolades for her work, including an MBE for services to education and community life, that continued until her passing in 2017.

A visible reminder of her legacy can be seen in Central Square, adjacent to the railway station. Created by sculptor Eve Shepherd, the distinctive bronze monument is a permanent tribute to Campbell's legacy and, at 4-metres high, stands as a beacon of hope and inspiration for future generations. The central part of the sculpture is her head and shoulders, perched on top of a tree trunk beneath which children have gathered to play and read. The work is rife with symbolism that hints at her dedication to teaching and learning, and a closer look will be rewarded with hints of her time in Tiger Bay. An especially intriguing aspect of the design is the

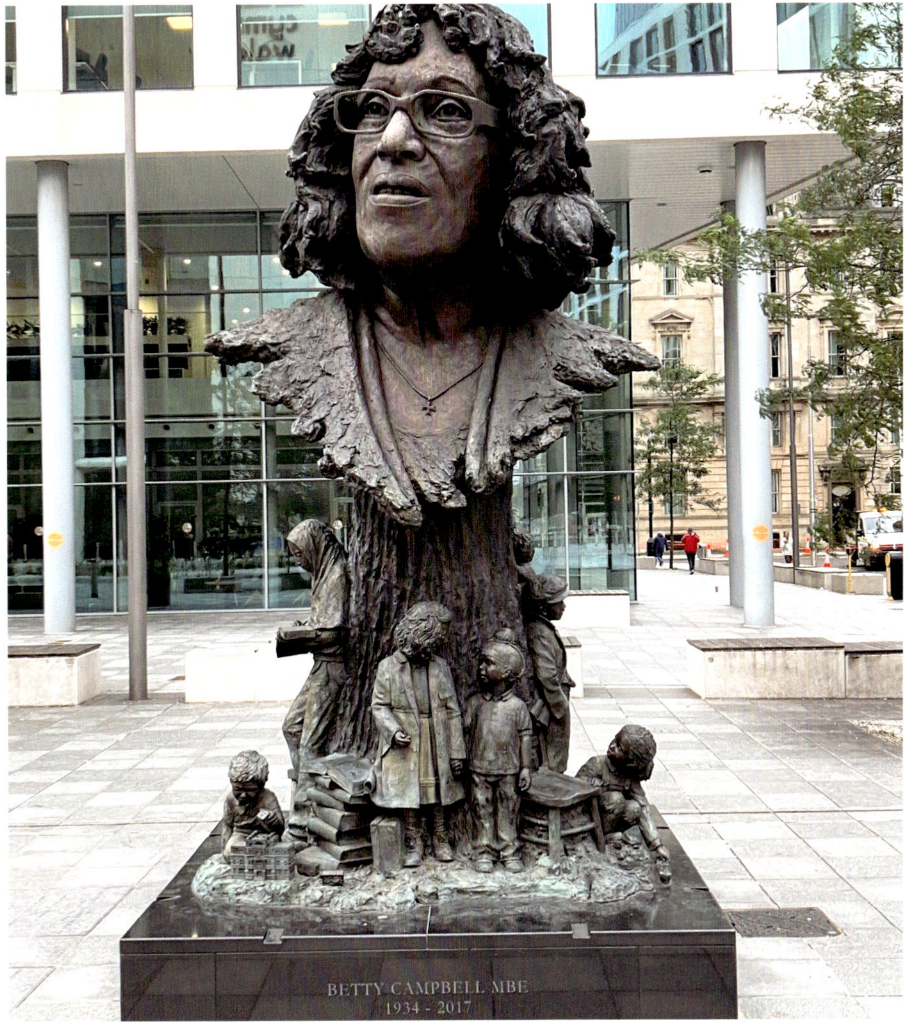

Statue of Betty Campbell in Central Square. (© DaHuzyBru (Wikimedia, CC BY-SA 4.0))

inclusion of an unoccupied chair and piles of books that might tempt children to enter the scene and engage with their sculptural counterparts.

Clara Novello Davies's Legacy

A statue outside Wales Millennium Centre stands, or rather sits, in memory of one of Cardiff's most famous sons: Ivor Novello. A strong argument could be made that there should also be one of his mother there too who, despite being less well known today, was also a hugely successful Atlantic-crossing star who lit up the stage and inspired future generations to achieve their dreams.

Clara Novello Davies was born in Canton on 7 April 1861. She was named after the acclaimed soprano Clara Anastasia, whose maiden name was Novello, and followed a similar path in life to her namesake. Davies sang in choirs from a young age, winning awards at the Crystal Palace contest under the baton of her father, the leader of the local church choir. She would go on to form her own ladies' choir, who sang across Britain before wowing in America, scooping the top prize at the World's Columbian Exposition of 1893, the first world's fair to be held in Chicago.

More than just a performer, Davies was a significant mentor who steered the careers of young singers. She published a guide to singing entitled *You can sing* (1928) dedicated to Ivor, watched as her students flourished in competitions and eisteddfodau, and opened a school for training singers in New York. Her choirs would receive invitations to perform far and wide to some of society's leading figures, raising significant amounts of money for good causes along the way.

Clara died at the age of eighty-one on 7 February 1943 in London at a time when her son began to find success with his stage musicals, with one of his biggest hits, *Perchance to Dream*, opening two years later. Ivor is perhaps best known for his wartime hit 'Keep the Home Fires Burning' (1914) and was an early convert to the silver screen, notably starring as a menacing figure in Alfred Hitchcock's first thriller, *The Lodger: A Story of the London Fog* (1927). He died in 1951, also in London, and four years later the Ivor Novello Awards were named in his memory. A blue plaque can be found on his birthplace on Cowbridge Road East.

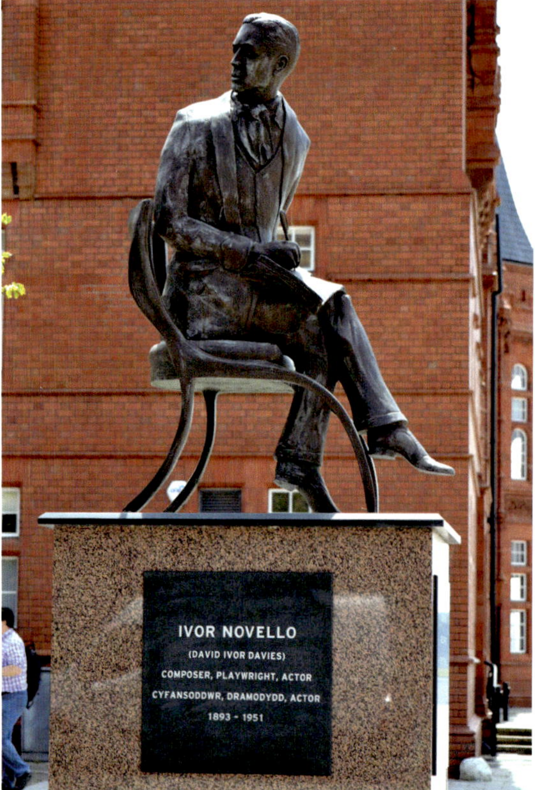

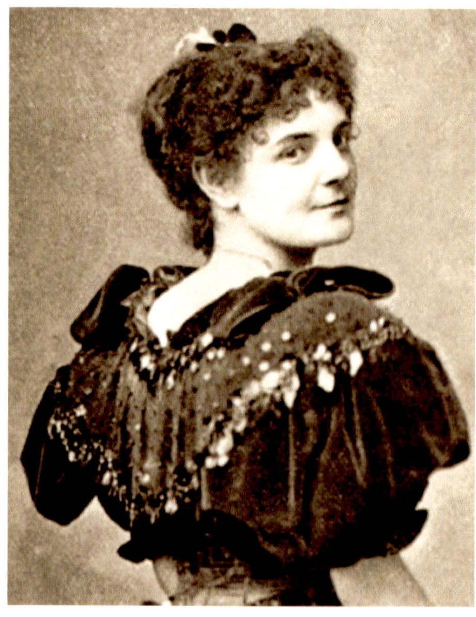

Above: Clara Novello Davies in 1896.

Left: Ivor Novello statue in Cardiff Bay. (© Elduendesuarez (Wikimedia, CC BY-SA 3.0))

Capital of Culture

Cardiff is both the capital and cultural heart of Wales. It's a city where tradition blends with innovation to create a place alive with creativity, celebrating its artistic legacy while embracing new ideas and diverse cultural life.

Music lies at the core of the city's identity. From the birth of Welsh opera, a dream made reality thanks to the work and dedication of passionate individuals, to the world's oldest record shop, which has welcomed music lovers for over a century, Cardiff's musical heritage is rich and varied. The bustling art scene further encapsulates the city's spirit of innovation, from masterpieces in national museums to cutting-edge street art that revitalises tired old buildings.

In this chapter, we embark on a journey through this cultural landscape, navigating the winding roads in search of hidden artistic gems.

The Humble Origins of Opera

Today, Welsh National Opera (WNO) is recognised as one of the most esteemed opera organisations in the world. However, many might not realise that this renowned company, which fills theatres across Wales, England, and beyond, began not as a professional entity but as a passionate group of dedicated enthusiasts who came together in Cardiff during the Second World War.

Wales's reputation as the 'land of song' emerged from the singing traditions of its churches and chapels in the nineteenth century. This communal passion for music led to the formation in 1943 of what was then known as the Welsh National Opera Company. Conceived by a group of friends led by singer and conductor Idloes Owen, who would become the first Music Director, they met in Cathays Methodist Chapel, and rehearsals began in January 1944. The original group of around sixty enthusiasts came from all walks of life, with amateur singers and students rubbing shoulders with shop workers, railway employees, a butcher and a publican.

Their first live recital was performed at the Empire Theatre that April, but the group had to wait until 1946 to stage their first full-scale opera at the Prince of Wales Theatre. It was all hands-on deck, with an orchestra assembled from local musicians, cast members sewing their own costumes, and the sets being tinkered with until the curtain raised. On 15 April 1946, the dream of a national Welsh opera company became a reality with a performance of the popular Cav/Pag double bill, which consists of Mascagni's *Cavalleria rusticana* and Leoncavallo's *Pagliacci*. Conducted by Owen, it featured the tenor Tudor Davies and soprano

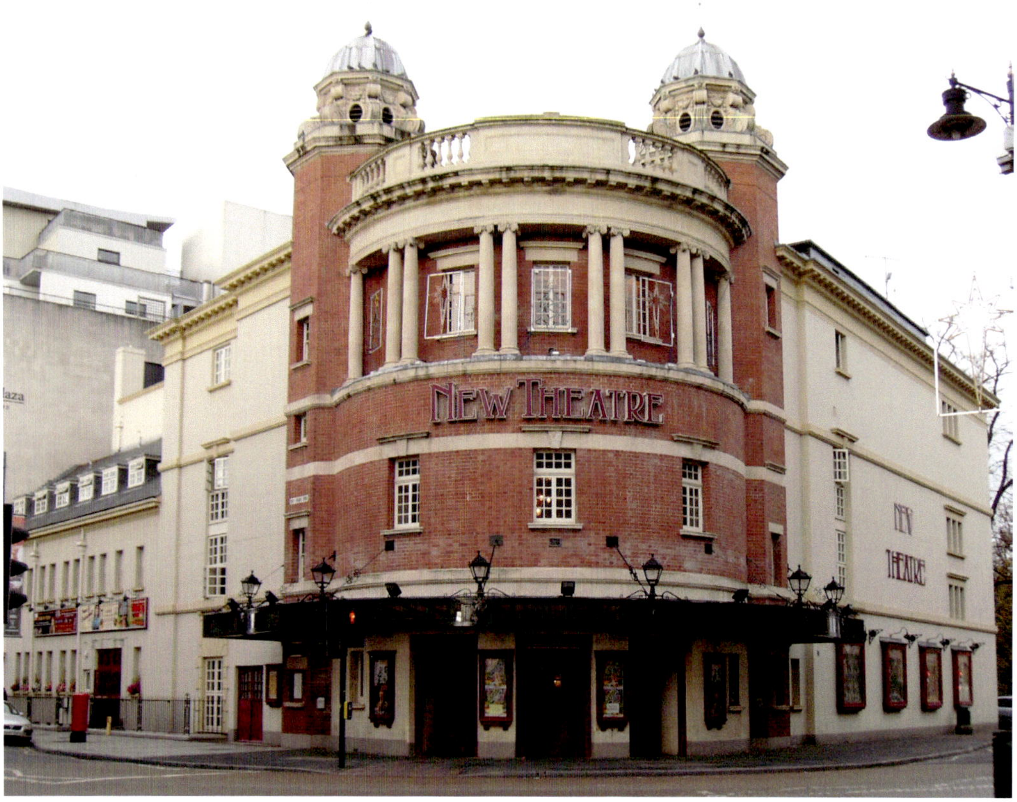

The New Theatre, the WNO's home for fifty years.

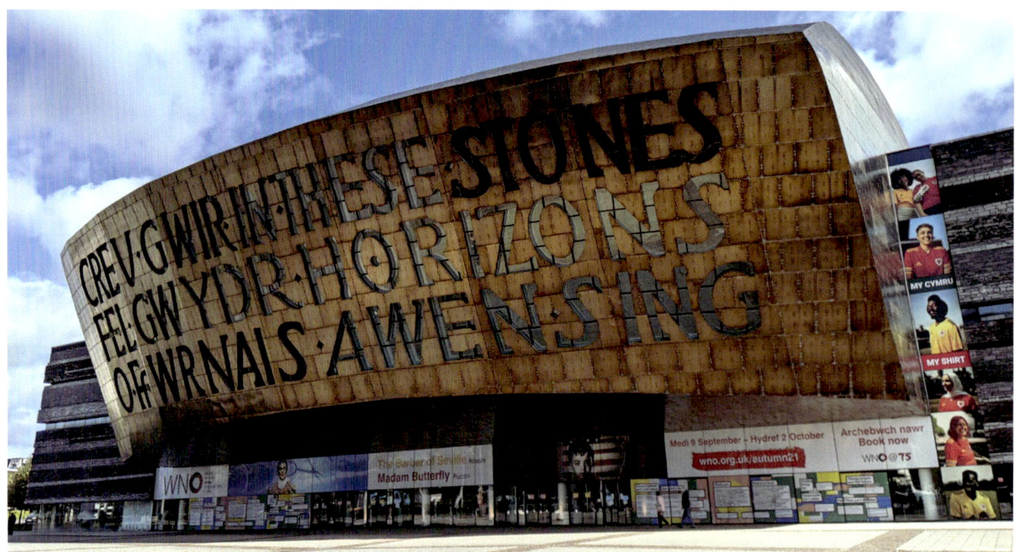

Wales Millennium Centre during WNO's Autumn 2021 season. (© Daniel (Flickr, CC BY 2.0))

Margaret Williams. The company further cemented their place in history in 1952 when they staged an epic performance of Verdi's *Nabucco* in the Sophia Gardens Pavilion, described as 'the first fully-staged production of this opera in the UK for a century'.

Two years later, the company settled in the New Theatre, an auditorium far better suited to their acoustic needs and equipped with an orchestra pit. They remained there for fifty years before relocating to the newly opened Wales Millennium Centre in 2004. This custom-built venue offered not only a cutting-edge performance space but also offices and rehearsal areas within the same complex.

Looking Better with Age

An incredible design feature of Wales Millennium Centre, Wales's national arts centre in Cardiff Bay, is that its exterior improves with age. Yes, with every day that passes, it looks a little bit better than the day before.

Having opened in November 2004, with BBC Hoddinott Hall added in January 2009, the Centre stages world-class opera, dance, and musical theatre productions. It boasts a distinctive copper-coloured façade that has led some people to call it 'the armadillo' due to its resemblance to the animal's shell. This 'armadillo shell', however, serves a practical purpose, as well as an aesthetic one. Situated in Bute Place, which can become something of a wind tunnel, it was devised to withstand the chilly ocean breezes that can cause havoc with even the sturdiest of architecture.

Designed by Jonathan Adams of Percy Thomas Architects, the spacious interior is populated with auditoriums of varying sizes, dotted with creative spaces, offices, shops, and bars. Tasked with creating a building that was both

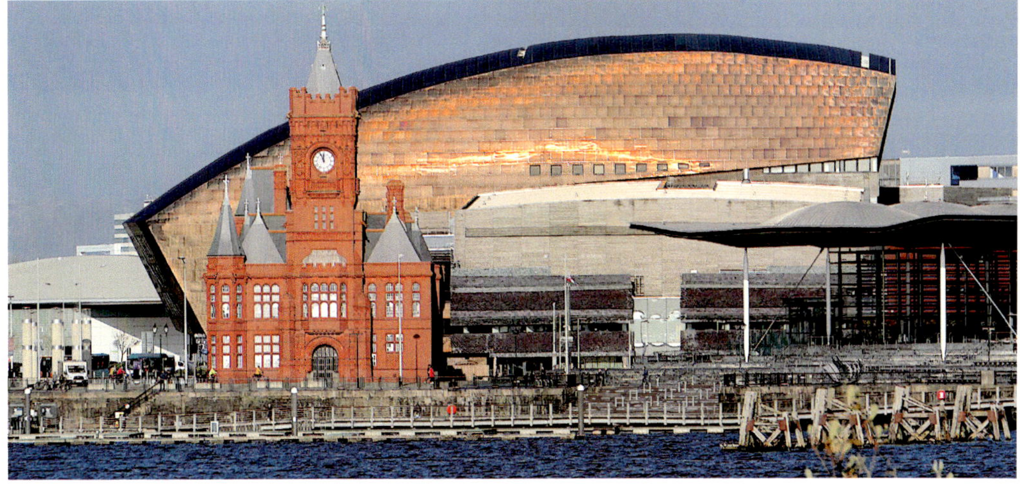

A side view of Wales Millennium Centre showing the 'armadillo' shell. (© Richard Szwejkowski (Flickr, CC BY-SA 2.0 DEED))

instantly recognisable and uniquely Welsh, many of the architectural choices reflect these concepts. This includes a Welsh slate lower exterior inspired by the multicoloured cliffs of Ogmore and Southerndown, and the illuminated bilingual calligraphy that looms over the entrance from Welsh poet Gwyneth Lewis. The Welsh reads 'Creu Gwir fel Gwydr o Ffwrnais Awen (Creating truth like glass from inspiration's furnace)' and the English 'In These Stones Horizons Sing'.

These words can be found on the most striking feature of the building, the steel-clad bronze dome that overhangs the entrance. As with the slate, the steel reflects the industry of Wales. Adams consciously designed it to include visible rivets and a rough texture to reflect the 'old industrial structures, such as those that used to be commonplace around the landscape of the industrial south'. By treating it with copper oxide, it will not only survive the rough winds that blow in from the sea but will also improve in appearance as the wild weather ages it.

The Oldest Record Shop in the World

A Cardiff musical establishment and haven for generations of music lovers proudly holds the title of 'the oldest record shop in the world'.

Established in 1894 by the visionary Henry Spiller, Spillers Records began its journey in Queen's Arcade, where it sold phonographs – the music-playing devices

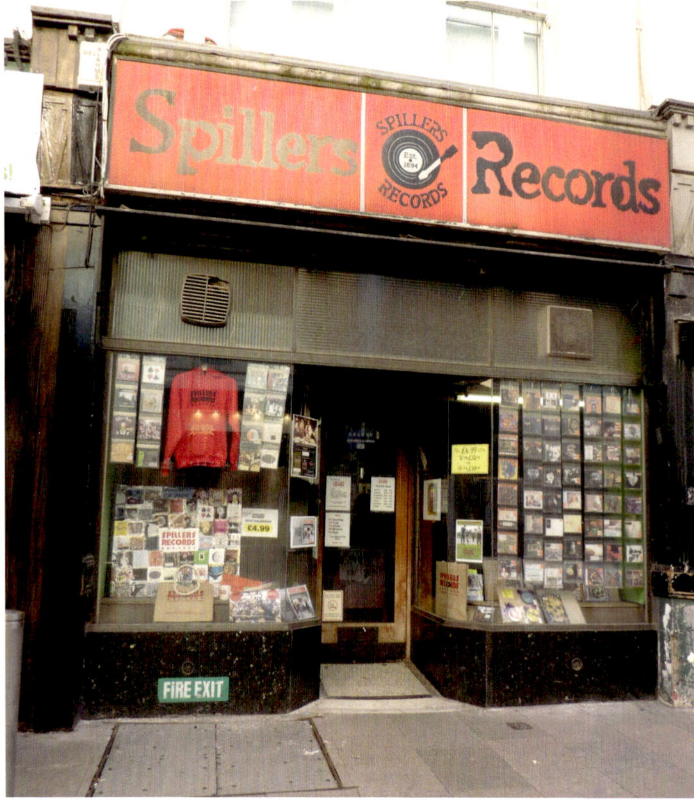

Spillers Records while in The Hayes, 2010. (© judyboo (Flickr, CC BY-ND 2.0))

of the time – and the cylinders and discs that contained the music. The shop soon expanded to include the sale and repair of musical instruments. Henry's son, Edward, took over in the 1920s, further broadening the shop's offerings. In the late 1940s, Spillers Records moved to a more expansive location on the Hayes.

Throughout the decline and subsequent resurgence in physical media sales in the twenty-first century, Spillers Records has continually reinvented itself. In 2006, it faced an uncertain future when a rent increase threatened its existence. However, a campaign led by the likes of the Manic Street Preachers, Columbia Records, and Owen John Thomas, the Plaid Cymru politician and a founding member of fellow historical Cardiff musical venue Clwb Ifor Bach, helped save this cultural gem.

In 2010, Spillers Records relocated to Morgan Arcade, initially as a temporary measure, but at the time of writing, it continues to trade in music from the Morgan Quarter. It also continues to welcome some of music's biggest names through its doors, from The Pixies to David Bowie, who visited shortly before his death in 2016.

The Parisian Lady

On 15 April 1874, the French art scene was rocked by a mixture of outrage and bemusement when a group of idealistic young artists, rejected by the establishment, staged their own exhibition of groundbreaking art. Paris, the heart of the art world, was where artists flocked to have their works displayed

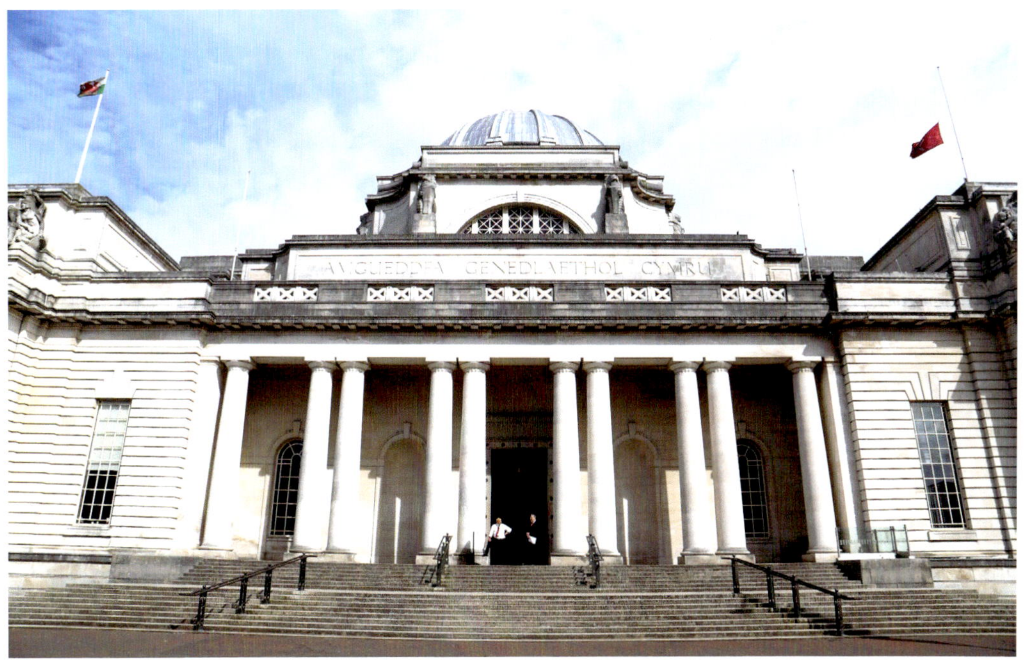

National Museum Cardiff. (© Senedd Cymru/Welsh Parliament (Flickr, CC BY 2.0))

at the official Salon, the gatekeepers of Parisian art. When a number of artists had their works declined due to the perceived unartistic nature of their art, thirty like-minded individuals banded together to stage their own exhibition. This group, who come to be known as the Impressionists, included many artists who are now household names, such as Cézanne, Degas, Monet, Morisot, Pissarro, Renoir, and Sisley. Today, their scenes of waterlilies, rowing boats, and carefree Parisians enjoying a drink and a dance are considered quaint, quintessential chocolate-box images; yet their rule-breaking techniques and painterly brushstrokes were highly revolutionary and controversial at the time.

The largest collection of these Impressionist works outside of France can be found in Cardiff. Arguably the showpiece of the collection and one of the most well-known paintings on display in Wales is Renoir's *The Parisian Lady (La Parisienne)*, which appeared at that very first exhibition. It was bequeathed to National Museum Cardiff in 1952 by Gwendoline Davies, who, along with her sister Margaret, contributed the majority of the Impressionist works now on display. The model is Henriette Henriot, a young actress and a favourite of the painter's, depicted as a modern, cosmopolitan woman decked out in the latest fashions. The work emphasises the clothing to such an extent that it feels more like a magazine advert than a portrait, and the deep blue drapery is intensified by the unusually empty space in which she appears to float. One of the reasons it was rejected by the Salon is its 'unfinished' appearance, a trademark of Impressionism which was very much at odds with the more precise technique expected of a French artist.

In 2024, one hundred and fifty years after that groundbreaking exhibition, *The Parisian Lady* returned to Paris temporarily as part of the Paris 1874 commemorations at the Musée d'Orsay. In return, they loaned a Vincent van Gogh self-portrait to National Museum Cardiff, which took centre stage at the nearly year-long Art of the Selfie exhibition.

The Senedd's Secret Art

Since its grand opening on St David's Day in 2006, the Senedd in Cardiff Bay quickly became one of the country's most recognisable buildings. The home of the Welsh Parliament in the former docklands area is an architectural landmark dotted with artistic finds both inside and out, such as the Merchant Seaman's Memorial directly outside that fuses the hull of a ship with a sleeping face, and the temporary exhibitions staged within. Some of these works, however, are more than just aesthetic additions and double up as practical works of art.

The building itself was designed with longevity and sustainability in mind by renowned Pritzker Architecture Prize-winning architect Lord Richard Rogers. Spanning 5,308 square metres, it was nominated for the Stirling Prize in the year it opened, and four new works of art were commissioned at a combined cost of £300,000. As with the building, these artworks were created with both looks and functionality in mind. They include Alexander Beleschenko's *Heart of Wales*, a 2-metre-wide dome made of blue and gold glass in the Siambr, and

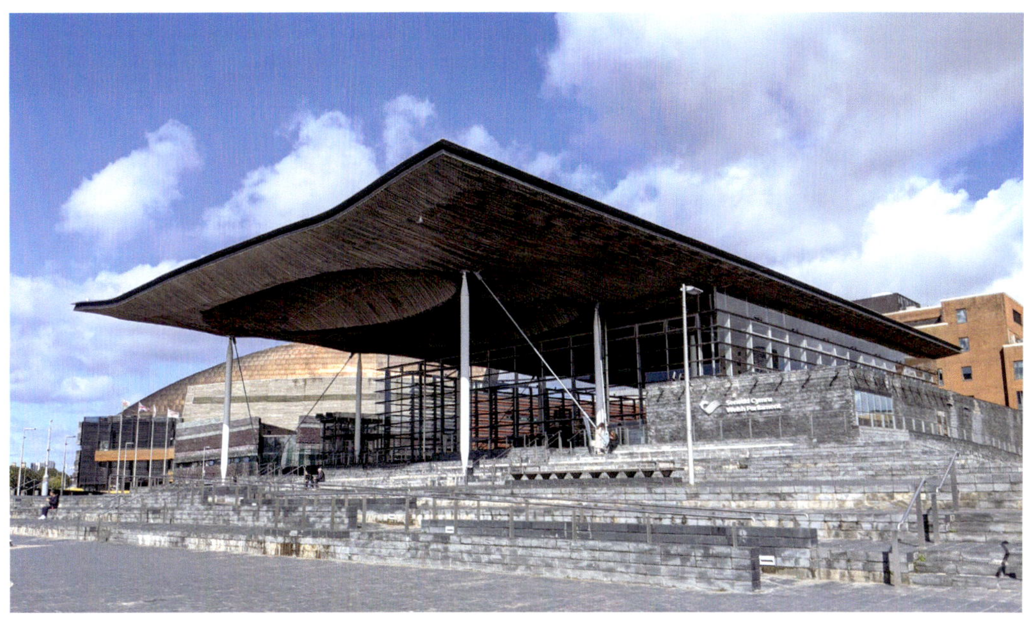

The Senedd. (© Daniel (Flickr, CC BY 2.0))

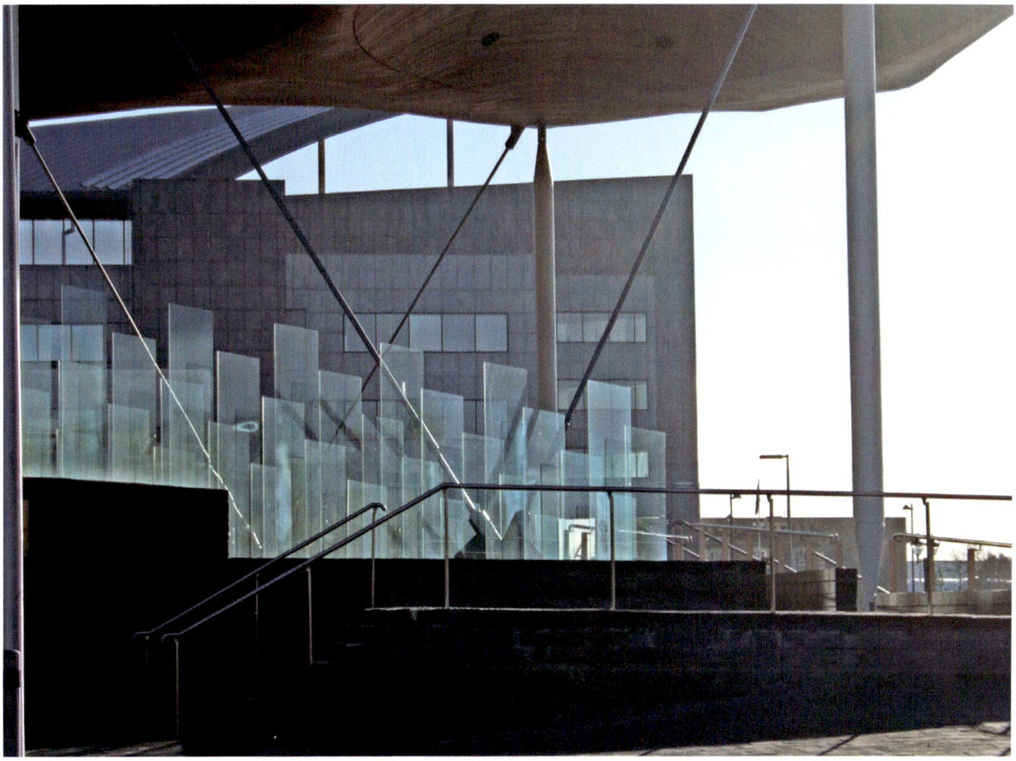

The Assembly Field outside the Senedd. (© plumandjello (Flickr, CC BY-SA 2.0))

Martin Richman's *Untitled*, which adds colour to the Senedd with hundreds of fabric-covered acoustic absorption panels serving both visual and acoustic purposes.

Outside, there are two creations that might be instantly familiar to Cardiff Bay regulars, though they might not necessarily realise their purpose. The first is *Assembly Field* by American glass artist Danny Lane, designed both to add flair to the front of the building and to shield the public from the gusty winds of the bay. Comprising five parallel rows of thirty-two vertical glass elements, each reinforced with sealant and varying in height, they add an interactive element to entering the building, giving the illusion of disappearing when viewed from different angles.

The second is *The Meeting Place on the Plinth* by Richard Harris from Devon, which, as the name suggests, was designed as a place where people could gather. Situated to the south of the Senedd, this curving sculpture was made from an enormous 45 tonnes of slate and stands as an inviting space for friends to meet or for a little quiet contemplation.

Inventing the Daleks

It's well-known that *Doctor Who* was successfully regenerated in 2005 by BBC Wales, but Cardiff's connection to the sci-fi series extends much further back to the very early days of the sci-fi smash. In fact, a man from Llandaff played a pivotal role in the show's mythology long before the successful revival: he created the Daleks, villains as iconic as the Doctor himself.

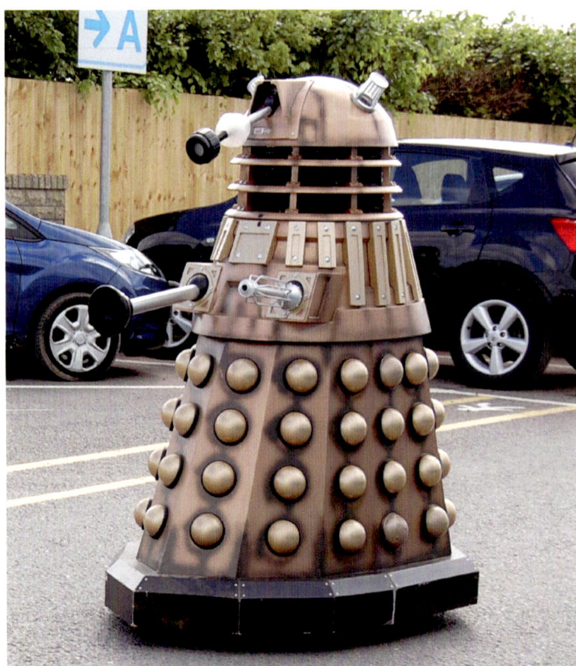

Exterminate! A Dalek spotted at Cardiff Airport. (© Holidayextras (Flickr, CC BY 2.0))

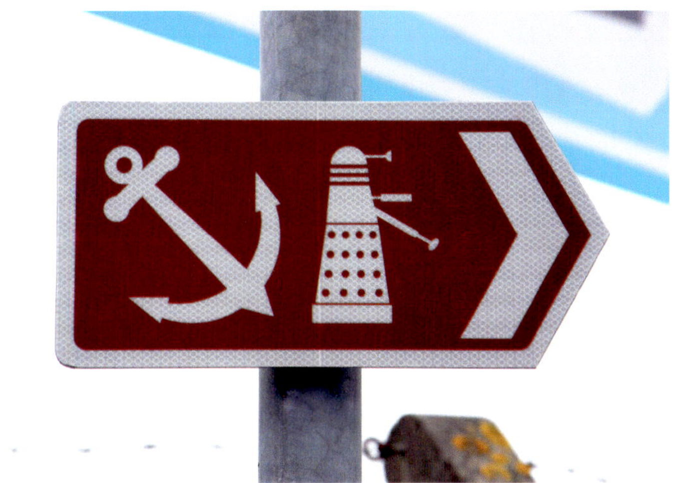

Directions to
the Doctor Who
Experience in
Cardiff Bay.
(© Chris Sampson
(Flickr,
CC BY-SA 2.0))

Screenwriter and novelist Terry Nation (8 August 1930–9 March 1997) began his career in comedy during the 1950s, writing for well-known personalities such as Eric Sykes and Frankie Howerd. In 1962 he gained his big break writing for Tony Hancock, though he parted ways after a disagreement. Later that year, Nation's career took a dramatic turn when he accepted a writing job on a new show called *Doctor Who*, having previously turned it down. Commissioning editor David Whittaker, impressed by Nation's work on ITV's short-lived Boris Karloff-led series *Out of this World* (1962), approached him to contribute to the series, and Nation responded with an outline inspired by twentieth-century totalitarian regimes, featuring an alien race driven by a lust for conquest.

It was snapped up and became the second serial to feature the first Doctor, William Hartnell, broadcast between December 1963 and February 1964. Simply titled 'The Daleks,' it was directed by Christopher Barry and Richard Martin, and the plunger-appendaged mutants were designed by Raymond Cusick. Nation revisited the Daleks multiple times, with his initial story inspiring the non-canon feature film *Dr. Who and the Daleks* (1965), starring Peter Cushing. As the copyright holder, he also ventured into new markets like comic books.

Nation's other notable sci-fi creations include *Survivors* (1975) and *Blake's 7* (1978), and he wrote for popular shows such as *The Saint* (1964–68) and *The Avengers* (1968–69). In 2013, during the Doctor Who 50th anniversary celebrations, a blue plaque was unveiled outside his former home in Llandaff, where he lived from 1930 to 1952.

Spectacular Street Art

In January 2023, Cardiff was gripped by outrage when a much-loved mural celebrating the city's multiculturalism was painted over with an advert for a watch company. The artwork on Quay Street, commissioned by Adidas in 2020 to

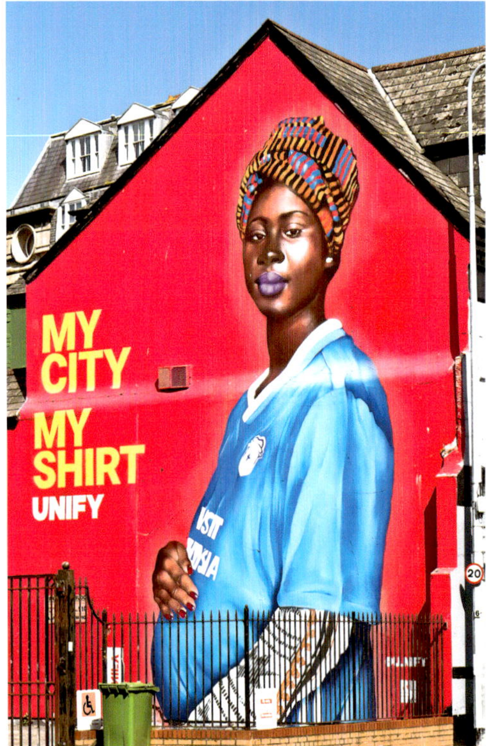

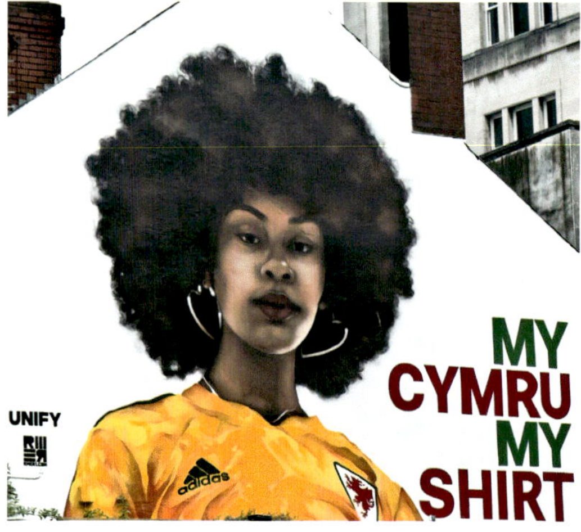

Above: UNIFY street art in Cardiff city centre. (© Andrew Rees (Flickr, CC BY-ND 2.0))

Left: UNIFY street art in Butetown. (© Andrew Rees (Flickr, CC BY-ND 2.0))

mark the Welsh football team's Euro campaign, had never been granted protected status, so no laws were broken – but many saw its removal as cultural vandalism, erasing a symbol of community pride.

Today, a new artwork has been created in its place, forming part of the UNIFY street art trail in the city, a Welsh creative collective fronted by Shawqi Hasson and Yusuf Ismail. Their works are large-scale, vibrant, and feature bold colours and catchy slogans, making them perfect for the social media age. Speaking to VisitWales, Ismail reflected on the lack of representation the duo experienced while growing up in the area, which now inspires their current work. They see their mission as bringing art to the public, removing the need to visit a museum to engage with it, and aim to create images that are 'very visible' and 'very representative of everything that's around us'.

The three works on the trail include: 'Butetown Mona Lisa' on James Street near the Wales Millennium Centre, a part of the national 'My City, My Shirt' campaign that celebrates diversity and inclusion in football; 'Gary Speed', a stone's throw from Cardiff City Stadium where Atlas Street meets Leckwith Road, featuring the words 'only one Gary Speed' in memory of the beloved Welsh captain and manager; and the recreated 'My Cymru, My Shirt' depicting the artists' friend Nicole, which is back on Quay Street in the city centre within easy walking distance from the Principality Stadium.

Brutalist Cardiff

The term 'Brutalism' was coined in mid-1950s England by architects Alison and Peter Smithson to describe a bold, raw aesthetic inspired by Le Corbusier's béton brut – a style that leaves its concrete exposed for all to see. This bold style featured large, unadorned concrete structures assembled in a way that starkly contrasted with the more refined architectural tastes that preceded it. Modern, edgy, and practical, it wasn't long before Brutalism was leaving its mark across Britain.

In post-war Cardiff, many of the city's most notable buildings were constructed in the Brutalist style. While opinions on its merits remain divided, its visual impact is undeniable. Noteworthy examples in and around Cathays include Cardiff Central police station at the corner of Cathays Park, designed by John Dryburgh in the late 1960s, complete with concrete planters; Cardiff University's Arts and Social Studies Library, designed by architects Faulkner-Brown, Hendy, Watkinson, Stonor in the early 1970s, who were known for high-profile leisure projects across Britain; and Cathays Park 2, also known as the new Crown Building, a five-storey office block and car park designed by Alex Gordon in 1979, a marked difference from the neoclassical Cathays Park 1.

A later example of Brutalism is the iconic St David's Hall, which was awarded Grade II listed status in 2023. It was designed with two main objectives: to

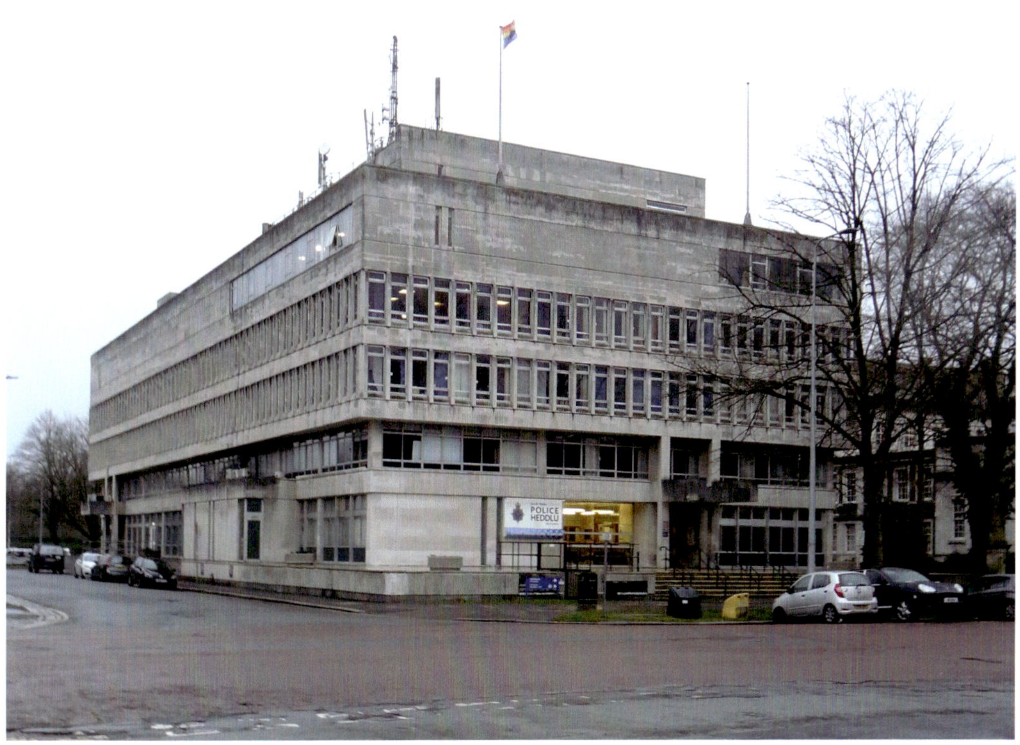

Cardiff Central police station. (CC0 1.0)

complement the adjacent shopping centre and to provide a state-of-the-art theatrical experience, especially in its concert hall, a feature Cardiff lacked as a modern capital. St David's Hall achieved this by combining Brutalist elements like concrete frames and staggered layers with a functional interior that democratically ensured all spectators had a good view. Today, it is recognised as one of the best venues globally for its acoustics and stands as a beacon of architectural excellence that enhances Cardiff's cultural landscape while respecting its historical context.

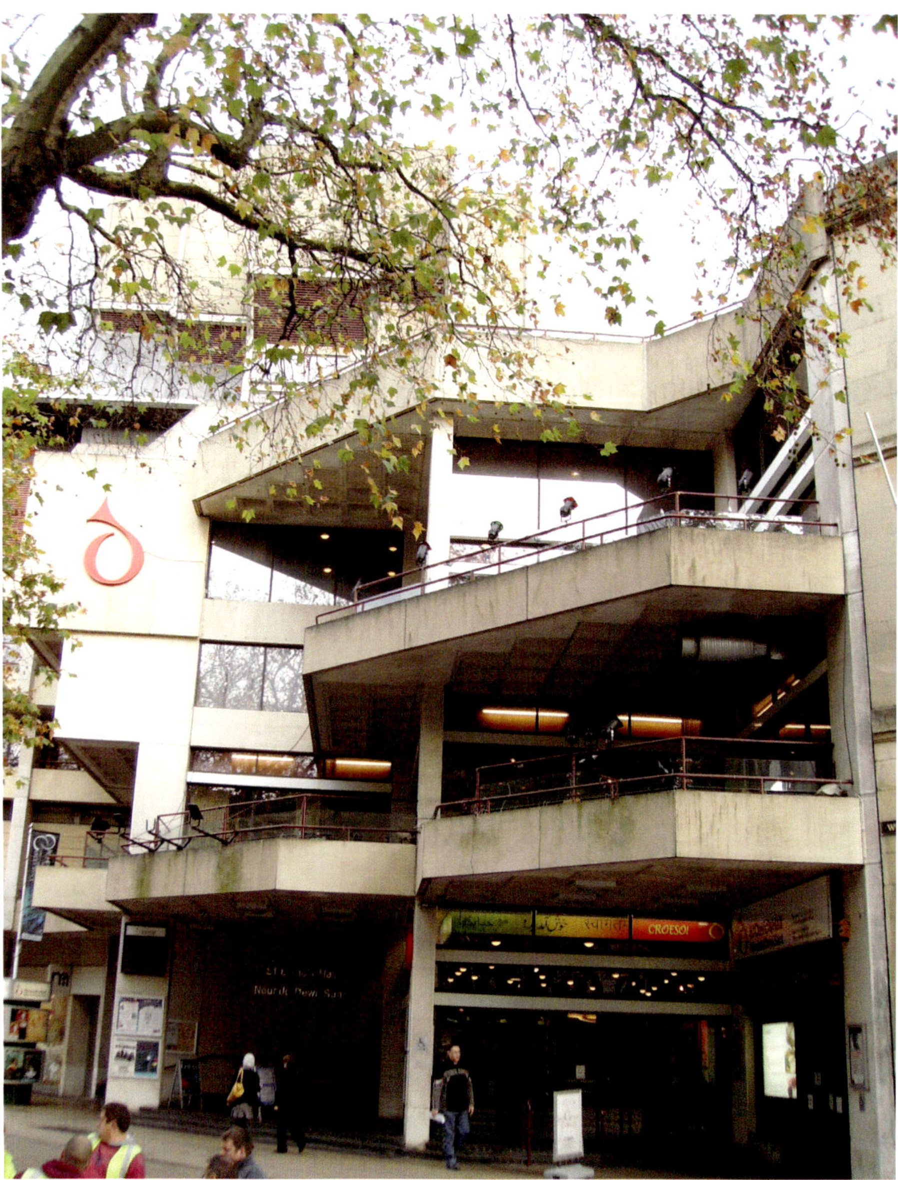

St David's Hall.

Law and Order

From brutal knife fights to headline-grabbing crime sprees, Cardiff's streets have borne witness to danger, bloodshed and the darker side of human nature. Lawlessness often clashed with those upholding justice, and it wasn't always clear which side was in the right. This is evident in events such as the Cardiff Bay race riots and the tragic fate of wrongly accused martyrs, exemplified by the story of Dic Penderyn, a symbol of the working-class struggle for justice in the face of oppression.

In this chapter, we delve into the darker aspects of Cardiff's history. These tales of crime and punishment are etched alongside the city's triumphs and tribulations, revealing a complex and sometimes grim past. Against a backdrop of poverty and prejudice, violence erupted on the streets, leaving a scar on the city's conscience and raising questions about the boundaries of tolerance and understanding.

Yet amidst the darkness, there are also stories of resilience and defiance, all contributing to the city's evolution into a capital. By confronting these ghosts of the past, we may uncover the enduring spirit of a city forged in gritty reality.

Cardiff's First Race Riot

By the 1840s, Cardiff's Newtown district was far from an integrated community. Irish immigrants faced suspicion and hostility from the Welsh, who believed that their acceptance of lower wages was depriving locals of work, pushing them into the workhouse. Exploited by employers and landlords, the Irish community lived in squalid conditions, which were believed to have contributed to a major cholera outbreak at the end of the decade.

This tension occasionally erupted into violence, exemplified by the death of Thomas Lewis, a popular Protestant Welshman from David Street, whose father owned the Red Lion Hotel. The altercation with John Connors, a Catholic Irishman, occurred near a Catholic church at the junction of the notorious Whitmore Lane and Stanley Street, resulting in Lewis succumbing to knife wounds. Although the specifics of the fight are shrouded in conflicting accounts, this outbreak, later known as the Newtown Riot of 1848, saw Welsh mobs target Irish homes and businesses.

Welsh mobs targeted Irish homes and businesses, and the police, unable to control the violence, faced criticism for their failure to promptly apprehend Connors. The press added fuel to the fire, and tensions further escalated during Lewis's funeral procession, when fresh clashes broke out. Connors was eventually captured in Pontypridd and tried at the Glamorgan Assizes. Despite rumours of a prior killing in Ireland, he was convicted of manslaughter rather than

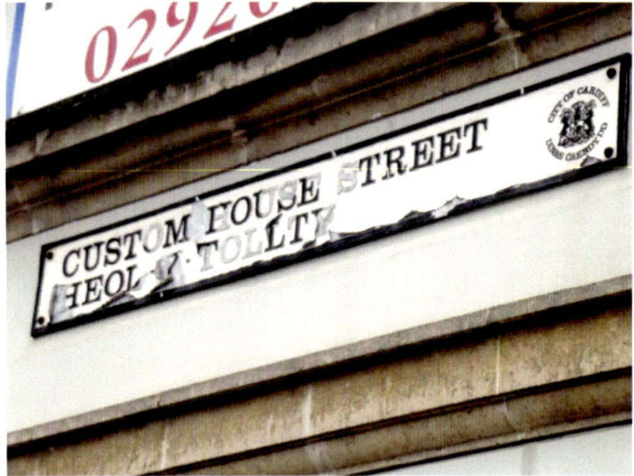

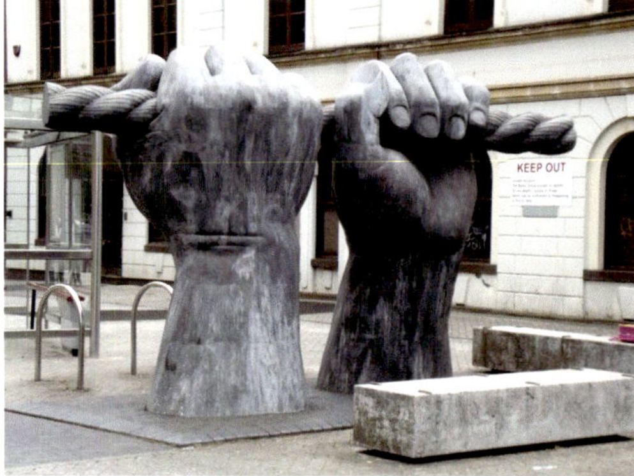

Above left: Custom House Street. (© Elliott Brown (Flickr, CC BY-SA 2.0))

Above right: *All Hands* by Brian Fell in Custom House Street. (© Elliott Brown (Flickr, CC BY-SA 2.0))

murder. The judge, stressing the necessity of proving intent, sentenced him to transportation to Botany Bay in Australia as a convict.

The area, now known as Custom House Street, is marked by a distinctive sculpture by Brian Fell. Made from galvanised and treated steel, it depicts two giant hands rising from the ground and clutching a length of rope, commemorating the canal workers who laboured nearby.

The Hollywood Psycho

In Alfred Hitchcock's chilling thriller *Psycho* (1960), Norman Bates, the knife-wielding maniac whose shadow on a shower curtain terrified audiences on the silver screen – and made a scream queen icon of Janet Leigh in the process – meets a fate that spares him from facing the justice system for his crimes.

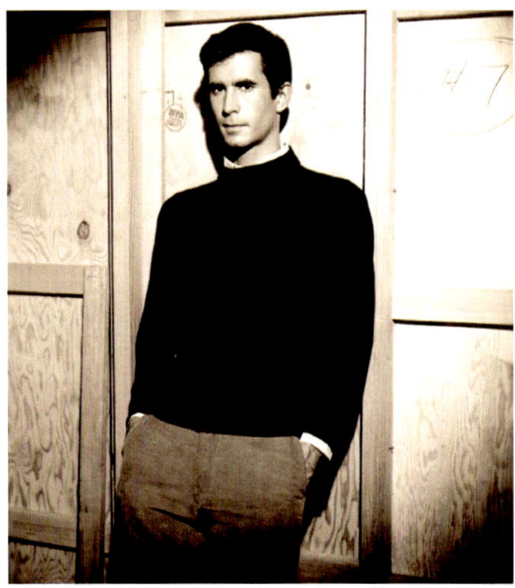

Anthony Perkins publicity photo from Paramount Pictures' *Psycho* (1960).

However, when the Oscar-nominated actor who so chillingly portrayed one of Hollywood's most infamous villains visited Cardiff, he couldn't outrun the long arm of British law and found himself standing before the Cardiff magistrates.

In 1989, native New Yorker Anthony Perkins, then fifty-seven years old, was in town to film several psychological mysteries for HTV penned by Patricia Highsmith, the author behind Hitchcock's *Strangers on a Train* (1951). He was staying at the Angel Hotel on Castle Street, and everything was going well until,

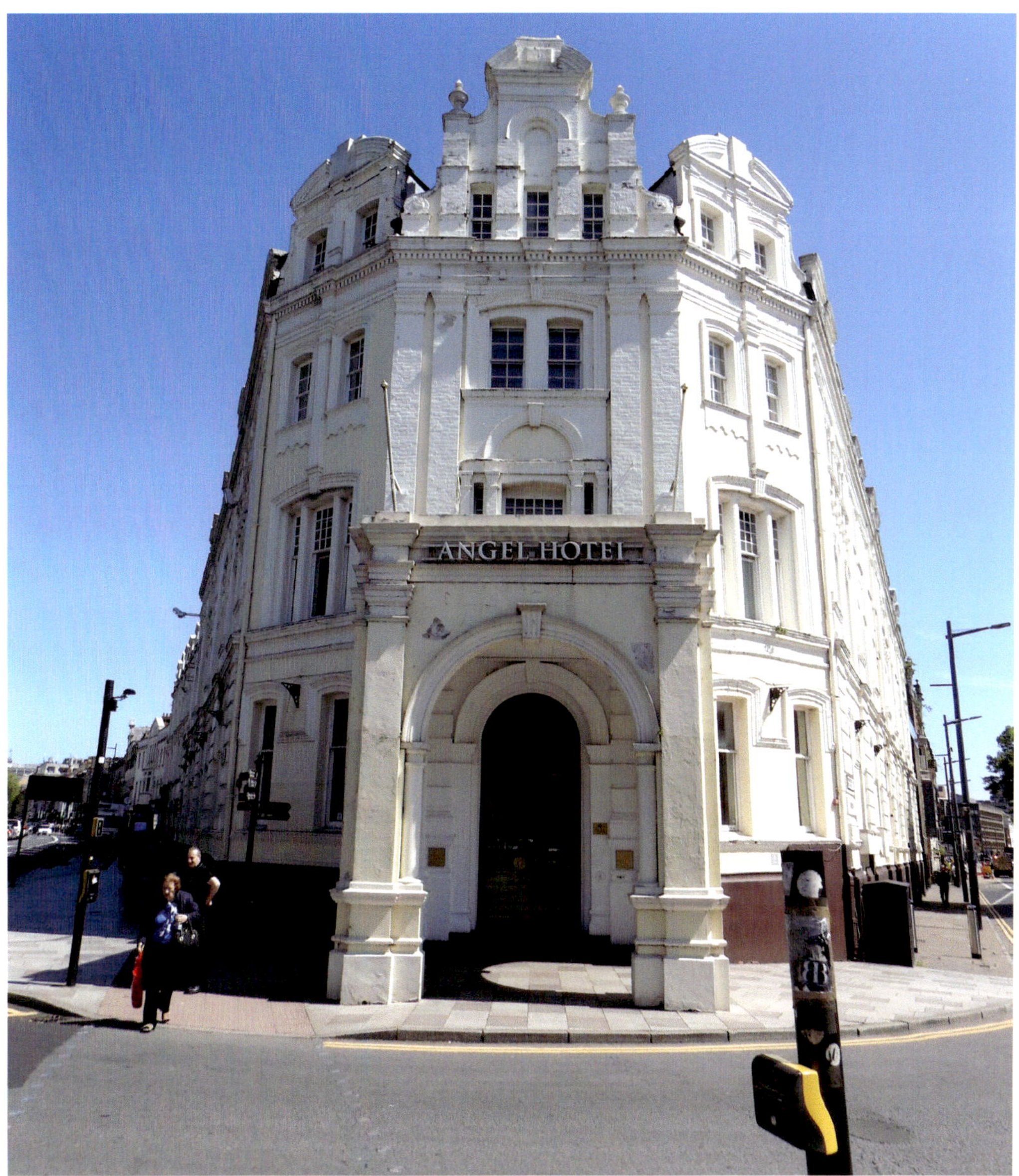

Angel Hotel. (© Reading Tom (Flickr, CC BY 2.0))

in a twist that might have been concocted by Hitchcock himself, a package of Perkins's personal belongings posted to the hotel from America went astray.

Unfortunately, it was not a package containing books, toiletries, or even underwear, but one containing homegrown cannabis that he had posted to himself from Los Angeles to avoid smuggling it in person – a seemingly foolproof plan had it not been for the fact that another Mr Perkins just happened to be staying at the same hotel and received the mail by mistake. When he opened it, he discovered 1.3 grams of a strange substance wrapped in foil and notified management, who then alerted the police.

Perkins's well-laid plan was foiled. Despite the relatively small amount of cannabis, valued at roughly £4.50 at the time, he admitted his crime and embarrassment at Cardiff Magistrates' Court and was fined £200 for his trouble.

Cardiff also has another link with *Psycho*. Ivor Novello's sinister performance in Hitchcock's first thriller, *The Lodger: A Story of the London Fog* (1927), as mentioned in chapter three, is said to have been the early inspiration for what would later become one of Hitchcock's masterpieces.

Death Junction

Death Junction is the eerie moniker given to the intersection uniting Crwys Road, MacKintosh Place, Albany Road, City Road, and Richmond Road in Roath. Despite the ominous nickname, it has nothing to do with car crashes or any kind of traffic chaos; in fact, its origins predate the invention of the motorcar and are

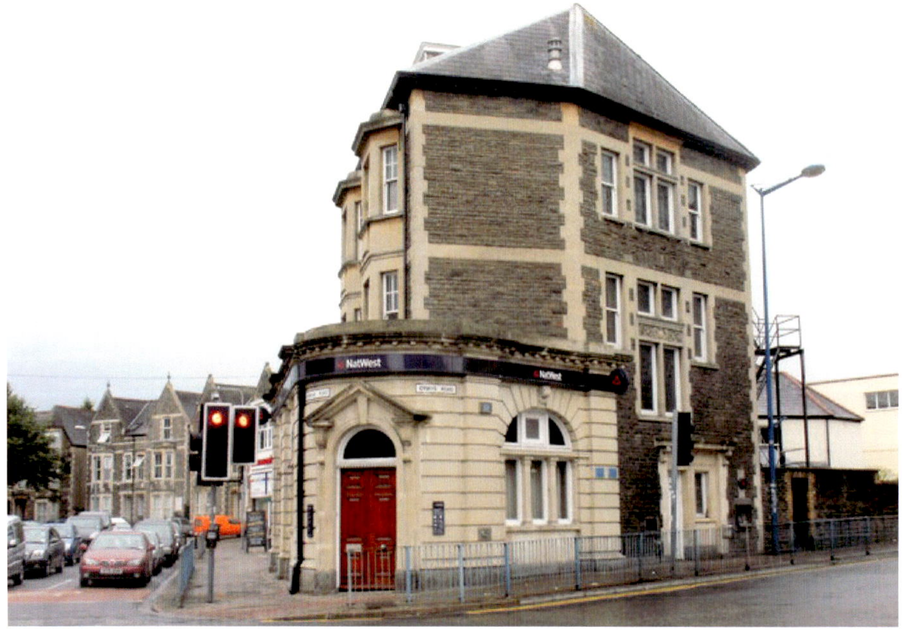

The NatWest building on the junction of Richmond Road. (© Jaggery (Wikimedia, CC BY-SA 2.0))

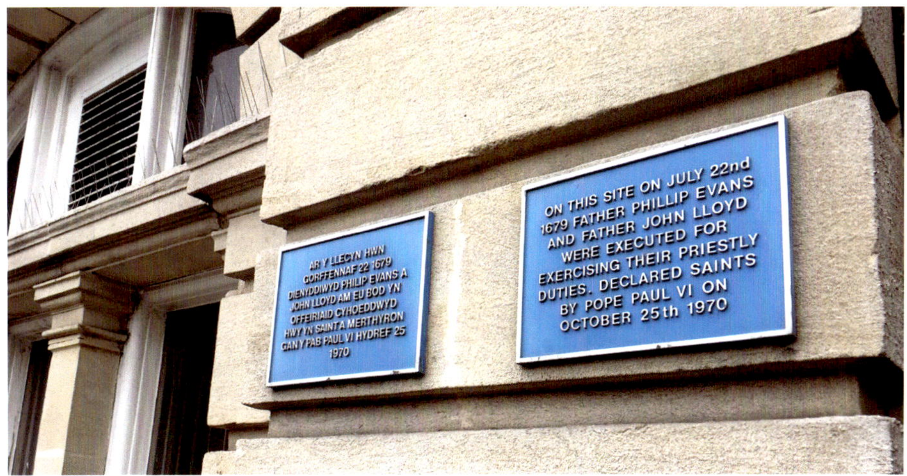

The plaques dedicated to Philip Evans and John Lloyd. (© No Swan So Fine (Wikimedia, CC BY-SA 4.0))

rooted in a dark historical event that led to the execution of two Catholic priests who, centuries later, would be canonised as saints.

In 1679, Philip Evans and John Lloyd were sentenced to be hanged, drawn, and quartered in Pwllhalog for practising their faith. Many other men faced beatings and whippings for refusing to testify against them. Before his execution, Evans addressed the crowd in both Welsh and English, bidding farewell to his fellow condemned priest with the words: 'Adieu, Father Lloyd! Though only for a little time, for we shall soon meet again.' Lloyd's speech was far more subdued, simply stating: 'I never was a good speaker in my life.'

They are remembered today as two of the Forty Martyrs of England and Wales, Catholic men and women executed for their faith between 1535 and 1679. They were canonised by Pope Paul VI on 25 October 1970, and their feast day is 23 July – a day after their execution to avoid clashing with the feast of Mary Magdalene. Plaques on the former NatWest building at the intersection of Crwys Road and Richmond Road bear silent witness to its macabre past, a stark reminder that, while it might be a bustling area today, it was once a regular site for hangings, which led to it becoming known as Death Junction.

Dic Penderyn

Dic Penderyn, one of Wales's most revered martyrs, was executed in Cardiff. Born Richard Lewis in Port Talbot, the labourer and coal miner became a prominent figure in the Merthyr Rising of 1831, a significant event in Welsh history marked by protests and demonstrations against oppressive working conditions and low wages in the iron and coal industries. When tensions between workers and authorities reached boiling point, clashes erupted between protesters and soldiers, and in the midst of the chaos a soldier was fatally stabbed.

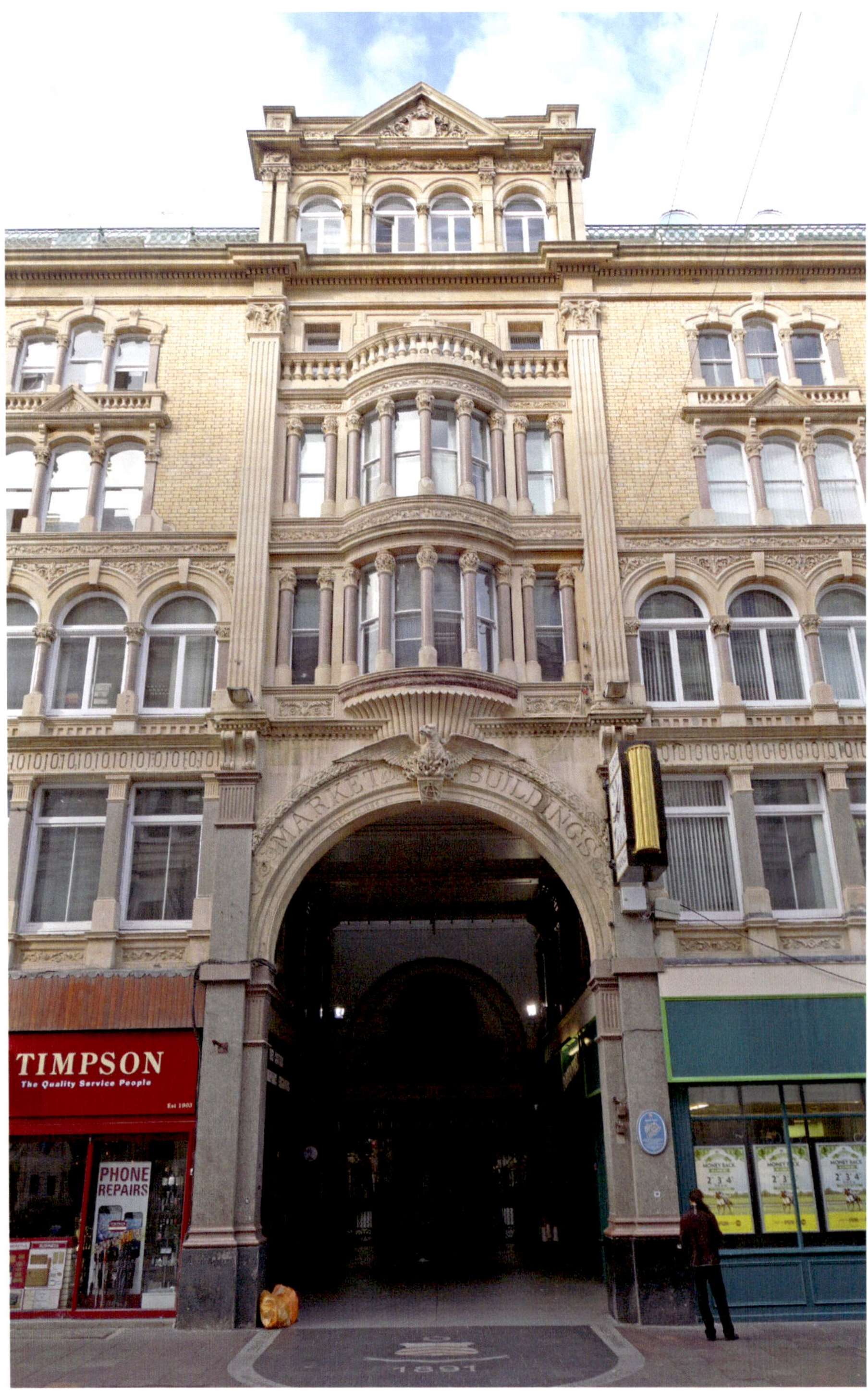

The entrance to Cardiff Market on St Mary's Street. (© Allie_Caulfield (Flickr, CC BY 2.0))

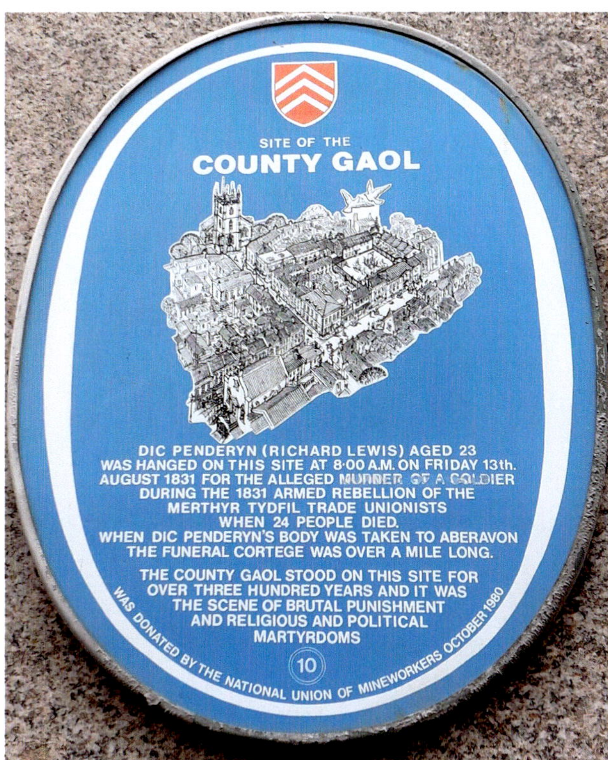

The Dic Penderyn plaque on the entrance to Cardiff Market. (Photo by Emma Hardy)

Despite a lack of evidence, Penderyn was arrested and accused of the crime. Thousands of people at the time, as well as many more in recent times, believe he was wrongfully accused and made a scapegoat for the authorities seeking to quell the uprising. Widespread public support and petitions for clemency did little to sway the verdict, and Penderyn was convicted and sentenced to death by hanging. On 13 August 1831, he was executed at the gallows outside Cardiff County Gaol, the location of which is now marked by a blue plaque on the entrance to Cardiff Market on St Mary's Street. It was here that he is said to have uttered his final words, which have entered Welsh folklore as a rallying cry for the labour movement: 'O Arglwydd, dyma gamwedd' ('Oh Lord, here is iniquity').

Following his death, his body was returned to Aberavon. The funeral procession stretched for more than a mile, and he is now buried in the churchyard of St Mary's. While the circumstances of his arrest and execution remain controversial, his story continues to inspire generations of activists and serves as a reminder of the ongoing struggles for fair treatment and equality in the workplace.

The 1919 Tiger Bay Race Riots

The race riots of 1919 cast a long shadow over south Wales. Three dark days in June of that year plunged Butetown into chaos and reverberated through the dock areas of Newport and Barry. With a shortage of work and housing following the end of the First World War, tensions flared between returning servicemen and minority communities. Violent clashes led to looting and fighting, resulting in the deaths of four people in the area, with similar unrest occurring in England and Scotland.

In Cardiff, the bustling port area known as Tiger Bay had become a melting pot of cultures, and it was there that white soldiers clashed with residents of predominantly Yemeni, Somali, and Afro-Caribbean descent. Beginning on 11 June 1919, the violence spread to Grangetown and parts of the city centre. For days afterwards, families from ethnic minorities were forced to barricade themselves in their homes to avoid the turmoil, which left behind bloodied bodies and shattered windows.

During this dreadful chapter, four people lost their lives, three of whom were in Cardiff. Mohammed Abdullah, a ship's fireman, was fatally injured in Butetown; John Donovan, a former soldier, was shot on Millicent Street; and Harold Smart was found with his throat slit, a gruesome discovery assumed to be related to the riots, although no witnesses were present. The fourth victim was Frederick Henry Longman, who was stabbed in Barry.

The aftermath of the riots exacted a heavy toll, both physically and financially. Hundreds were injured, and the extensive damage cost Cardiff Council £3,000. Despite the challenges, including racial biases that led to a disproportionate number of arrests of ethnic minorities and harsher court treatment, the resilience of the communities endured, highlighting a spirit that persisted in the face of adversity.

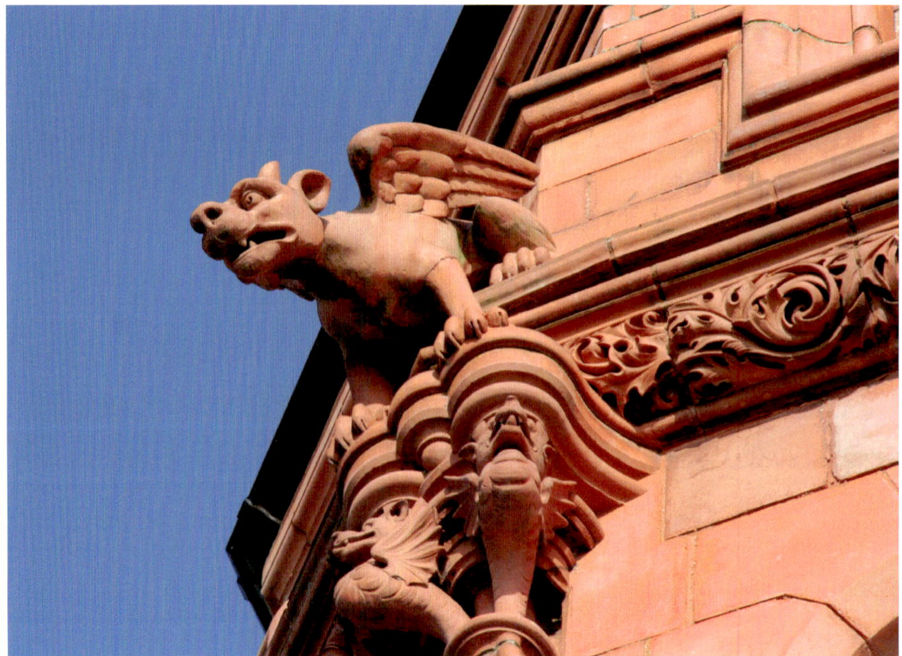

A dragon gargoyle looks out over Cardiff Bay from the Pierhead Building. (© Tony Hisgett (Flickr, CC BY 2.0))

Pirate of the Caribbean

Captain Morgan is perhaps best known today as the flamboyant pirate grinning back from rum bottles, or as a life-size statue outside bars promoting his spicy tipple. Yet long before these alcoholic associations, Sir Henry Morgan was a real 'Pirate of the Caribbean' – and Welsh, hailing from Cardiff or very nearby. The birthplace of Henry Morgan (*c.* 1635–88), born Harri Morgan, is believed to be Llanrumney Hall in east Cardiff, with Pencarn, just outside the city, as another possibility. Though records of his early life are frustratingly scarce, he retained a lifelong connection to south Wales, occasionally corresponding with friends back home, and is said to have named one of his Jamaican estates Llanrumney, likely in fond memory of his birthplace.

A ruthless adventurer, Morgan sailed the treacherous waters of the Spanish Main. In 1668, he led a raid on Porto Bello, slaughtering the garrison and looting the town, before mounting his famous overland attack on Panama City in 1671. Tales of his exploits – bold, cunning and often brutal – quickly spread across the Caribbean and back to the British Isles, cementing his notoriety. His fierce reputation earned him a knighthood from Charles II in November 1674 and the post of lieutenant-governor of Jamaica, where he remained for the rest of his life.

Morgan was also partial to a glass of rum, importing and profiting from Jamaican brandies and rums rather than distilling them himself. Local legend has it that his exploits inspired seafarers and would-be adventurers throughout Wales, keeping the memory of a Cardiff-born buccaneer alive for generations.

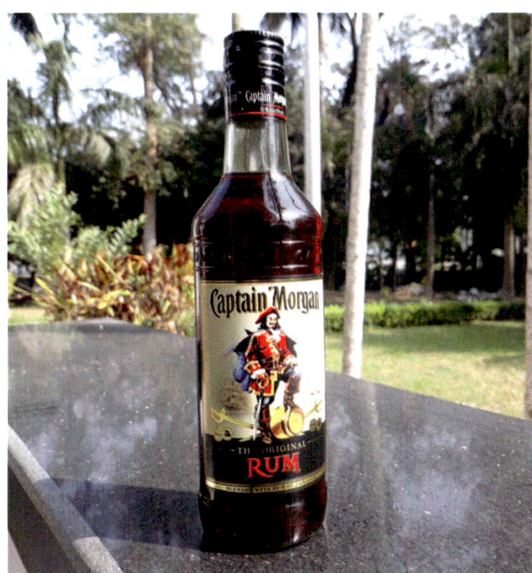

Above: A bottle of Captain Morgan rum. (© Pinakpani (Wikipedia, CC BY-SA 4.0))

Right: A Captain Morgan advertising statue at Wrigley Field baseball stadium in Chicago, USA. (© Steven Miller (Wikipedia, CC BY 2.0))

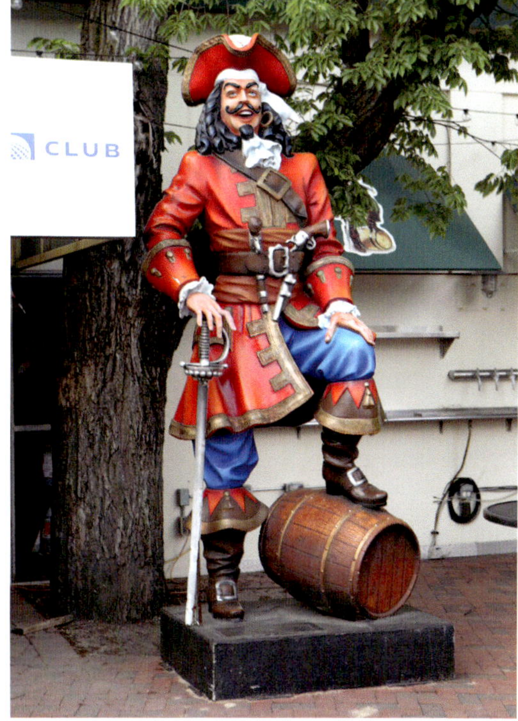

The Blue Anchor Murder

In October 1893, a chilling murder described by the press as a 'ghastly spectacle' stunned the people of Cardiff when two bodies were discovered at the Blue Anchor Hotel. They were found together in the main bedroom of the former drinking establishment, which was established in 1711 on St Mary Street. Reports indicated they were the landlord, David Jones, who had taken his own life after fatally shooting his wife Jane in her sleep.

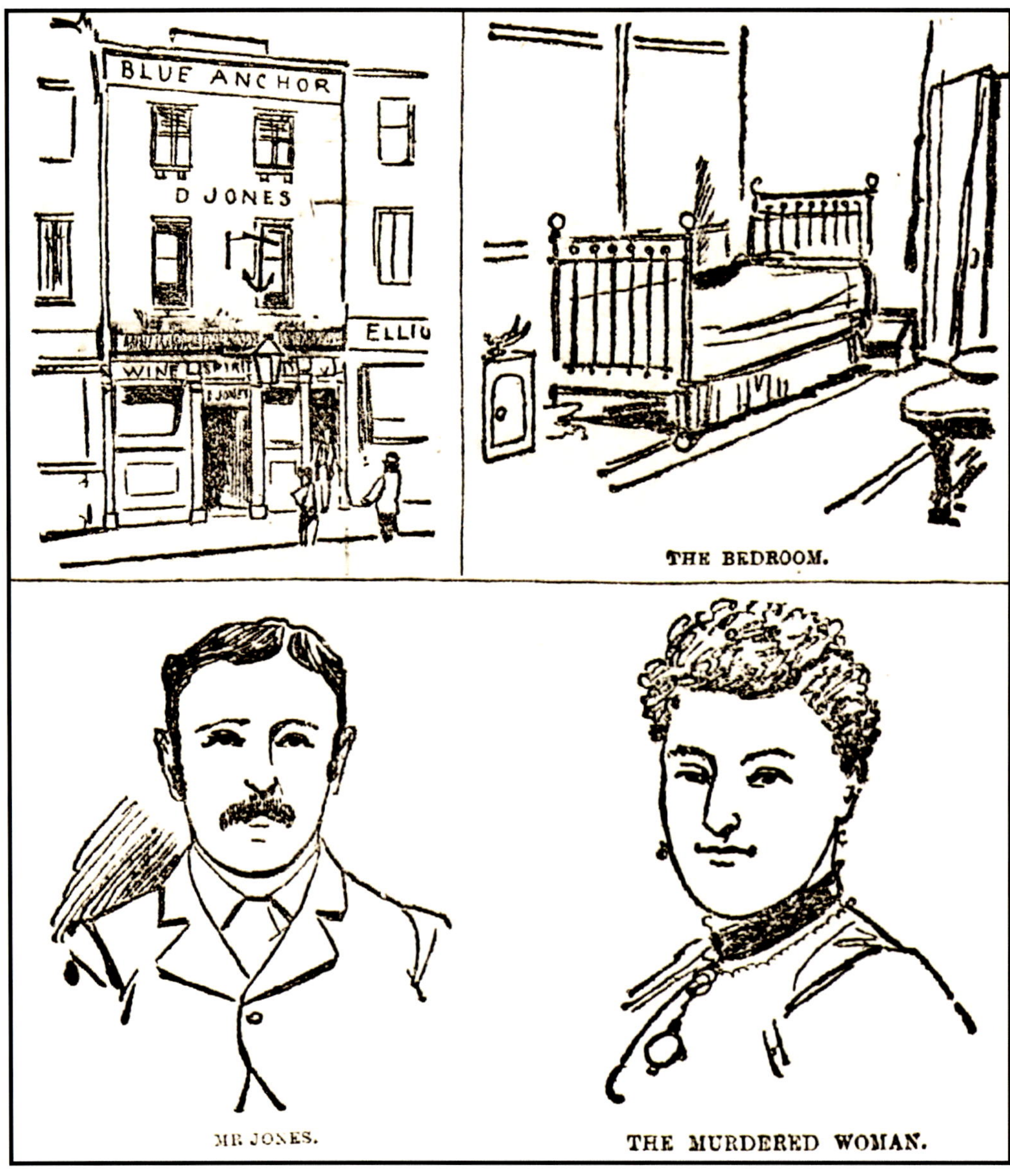

Newspaper illustrations from the Blue Anchor murder report in 1893.

Although the crime itself was not witnessed, substantial evidence pointed to Jones as the perpetrator. The tragedy came to light when the landlord's bedroom remained unresponsive to knocks from the servant and the barman, William Quick, who arrived for work around 8.30 a.m. Concerned by the silence, they forced entry and were met with a room filled with smoke and flames. Inside, they found Mr Jones dead from a gunshot wound and his wife severely burned and also shot. Quick extinguished the fire and alerted the police. Initial speculation about an accidental fire was dismissed by the presence of blood and a discharged shotgun, which pointed towards a murder-suicide.

Investigations revealed that the Joneses were facing both financial difficulties and health problems. While Mr Jones was praised for his sporting abilities and hospitality, he was also described as having a 'very uncertain temper'. The motive behind the tragedy was presumed to be a combination of financial strain, illness, and potential mental distress.

As news of the crime spread, a crowd of neighbours and onlookers gathered, turning the scene into a macabre attraction where curiosity mixed with sorrow. Those interviewed by the press suggested that the couple appeared to have a harmonious relationship, countering theories of jealousy or marital discord. This further reinforced the belief among bewildered friends and family that the incident stemmed from personal issues like financial troubles or deteriorating health.

Cardiff's Bullring

At the western end of Queen Street, a distinctive statue of one of Wales's most iconic figures stands on the site where a gruesome blood sport once made the city streets run red. Erected in 1987, the bronze likeness of Aneurin Bevan, sculpted by Welsh artist Robert Thomas, depicts Bevan pointing down from a prominent plinth that highlights his most notable achievement: 'Founder of the National Health Service'. However, long before Bevan's contributions to healthcare, this very spot was the site of much suffering and death.

The statue is surrounded by relics of a bygone era, such as the castle that looms behind it. Thankfully, the eighteenth-century bullring has long since been consigned to history. While its name today might suggest a modern shopping centre, the cruel spectacle of bullbaiting involved restraining the animal, usually by tethering it to a pole, so that it could be attacked by dogs until, more often than not, it was killed. This brutal pastime attracted large crowds and could also be perilous to those watching; in 1773, an onlooker was fatally gored by the bull.

Some defenders of this inhumane practice claimed it made the meat taste better, but bullbaiting was legally ended across Britain by the Cruelty to Animals Act of 1835. The practice was condemned not only for its cruelty to the animals but also for the public disturbance it caused. Its abolition was a welcome relief for the city.

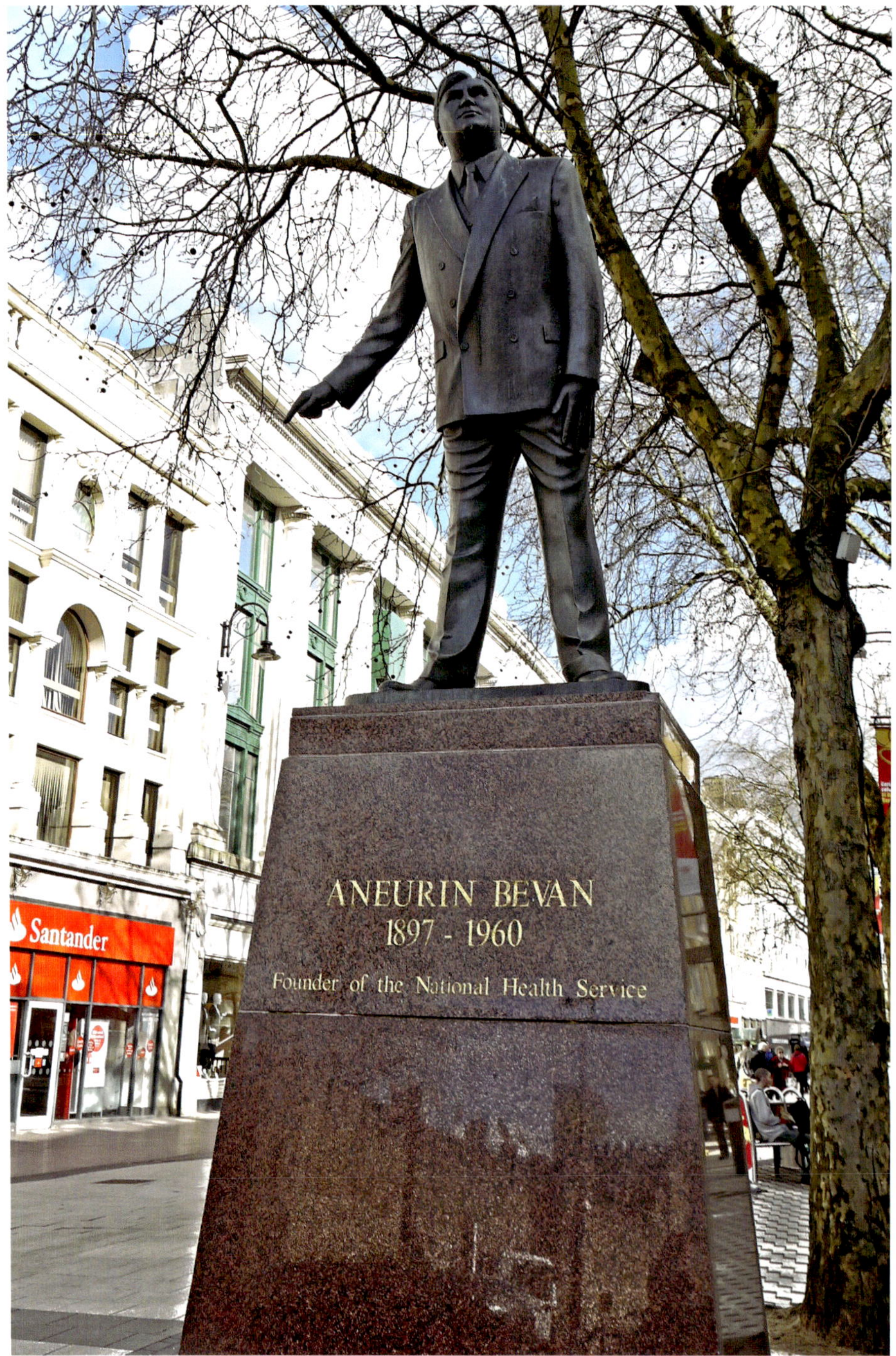

Statue of Aneurin Bevan on the former site of Cardiff's bullring. (© It's No Game (Flickr, CC BY 2.0))

Weird and Wonderful

When it comes to truly quirky history, Cardiff is home to many peculiar phenomena that mix fact and fiction, blurring the line between folklore and reality.

Some of these accounts are fantastical, steeped in literature and seemingly lifted straight from the pages of a fairy tale or *The Mabinogion*. For example, while Wales is well-known for having a red dragon on its flag, could there also be one lurking in the forests of the county?

Other accounts are far more haunting, from a headline-grabbing poltergeist to a famous séance that attracted celebrity ghost hunters. Many of these entries could be real-life cases for Mulder and Scully, and while the X-Files might never have investigated Cardiff, the city had its own paranormal investigators in the form of Torchwood, with one special member immortalised in Cardiff Bay.

In this chapter, we step into the unknown with tales that truly defy belief, starting with one of the strangest of all …

The Blood-Sucking Bed

One of the more unusual Cardiff legends concerns a peculiar piece of furniture that allegedly drank human blood like a vampire. In the early seventeenth century, a local family acquired the bed at a bankruptcy sale and placed it in their guest bedroom. The heavy four-poster bedstead seemed innocuous at first but quickly revealed its sinister nature when the lady of the house and the couple's newborn baby spent a few nights there due to a damaged floor in their room. The baby suddenly grew inexplicably ill and increasingly restless each day until it died with a mysterious mark on its neck.

Initially, the baby's agitation and subsequent passing were attributed to unknown causes. However, when the father, who needed rest following the birth of the couple's next child, slept in the guest bedroom, he too felt something clutching his throat, leaving a similar mark to the child's. Alarmed, he asked a friend to spend a night in the room, who reported experiencing the same sensation. Consulting an expert in the occult, they learned the horrifying truth: the bed was a vampire bed, a cursed artifact believed to drain the life force of those who slept in it.

Rather than destroying the bed, the man chose to keep it as a macabre curiosity, perhaps unable to part with the tangible evidence of his family's tragedy.

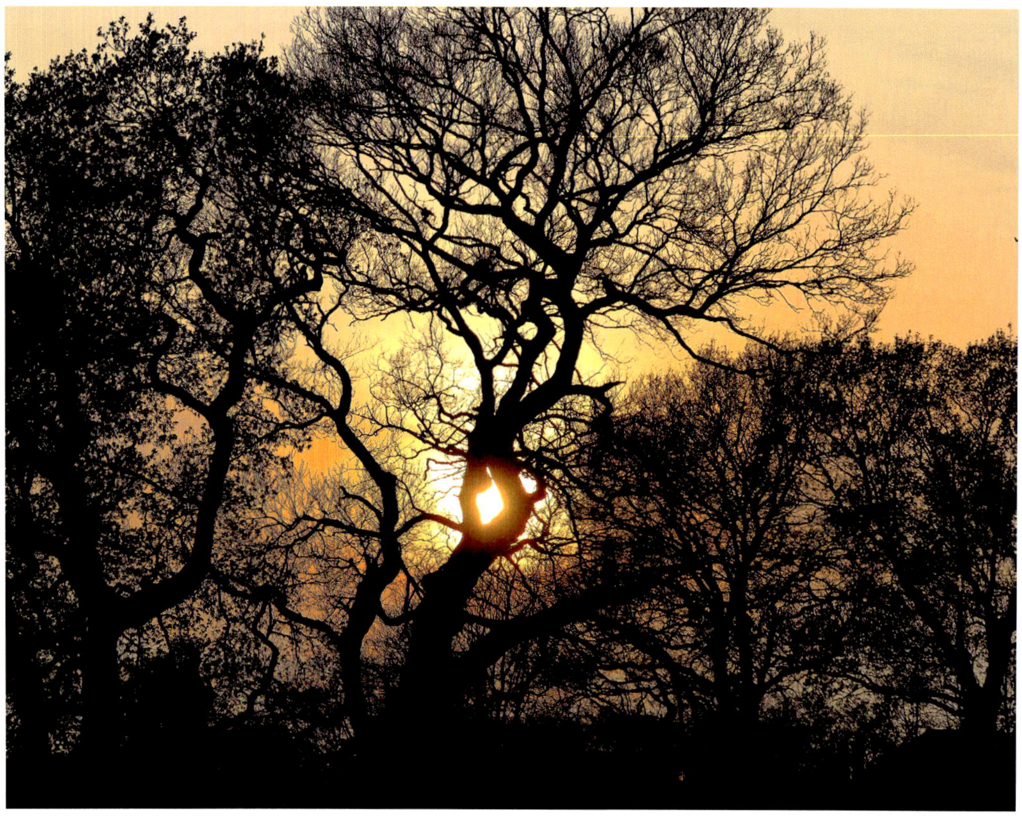

The sun sets in Cardiff. (© Richard Szwejkowski (Flickr, CC BY-SA 2.0))

The whereabouts of the vampire bed today are unknown, and if it still survives, it may be lying in wait in a spare bedroom somewhere in Cardiff.

Wales's 'Roswell'

In the early hours of 26 February 2016, locals in south Wales reported unusual aerial activity above Pentyrch – an incident later dubbed 'Wales's "Roswell"' by the press. At the time, it was unexpected and inconvenient, but hardly the kind of story anyone would have thought to remember years later – let alone include in a book. Officially, the military stated that the activity was part of Exercise Chameleon, an annual UK-wide Army and RAF training drill, but some witnesses remain unconvinced, suggesting that the true events of that night might have been covered up – and perhaps even had an extraterrestrial explanation.

Speaking to WalesOnline, witness Caz Clarke recalled seeing a green UFO release smaller red crafts, which formed an enormous triangle. The objects were reportedly pursued by military aircraft before disappearing behind the trees. Other locals described unusual explosions, shaking buildings, and mysterious figures in the area.

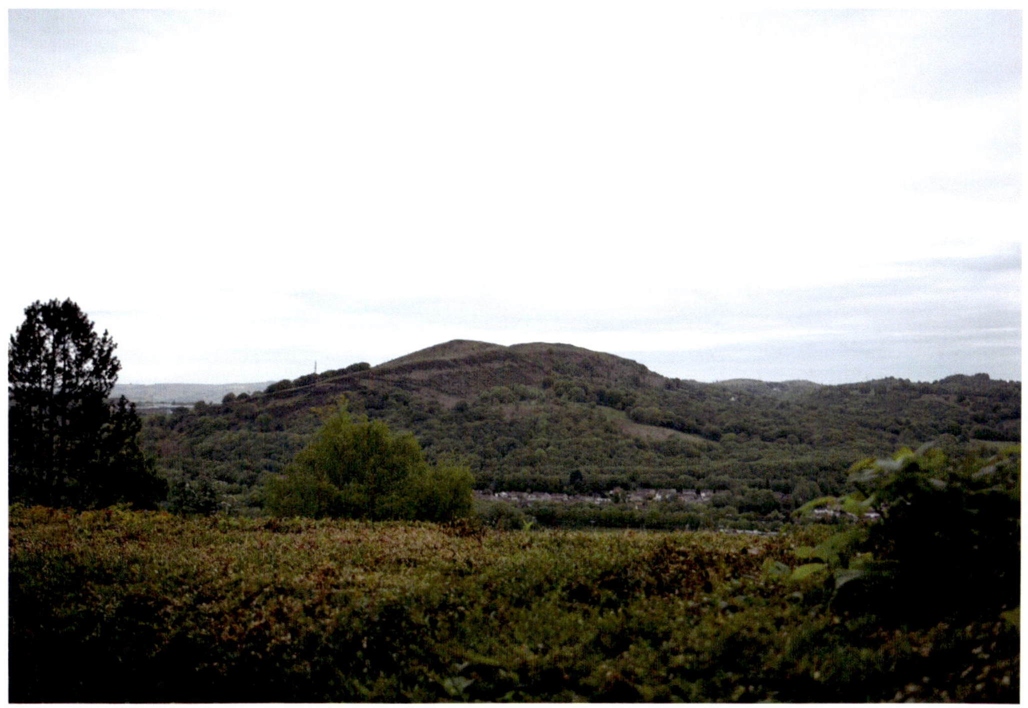

The Garth Mountain. (© Haydn Blackey (Flickr, CC BY-SA 2.0))

The Swansea UFO Network investigated from the top of Garth Mountain, which overlooks the site, and reported detecting electromagnetic residue at the core location of the sightings. Co-founder Emlyn Williams said: 'It's physical evidence something unusual happened there.' While sceptics point to a routine training exercise, the combination of vivid eyewitness accounts, the triangle-shaped formation, and lingering EM anomalies has ensured that the Pentyrch incident remains one of Wales' most intriguing modern mysteries.

The Dragon in the Woods

Wales is synonymous with dragons, thanks in no small part to the winged creature proudly displayed on the country's flag. This association with the red dragon (ddraig goch) dates back through the mists of time, with Welsh legend describing a battle between a red and a white dragon over the skies of Britain. The red dragon symbolised the native British people, and the white dragon represented the invading Saxons. While the white dragon initially appeared to be winning, it was prophesied that the red dragon would rally and triumph in the end, potentially embodied in the figure of Britain's greatest hero, the legendary King Arthur.

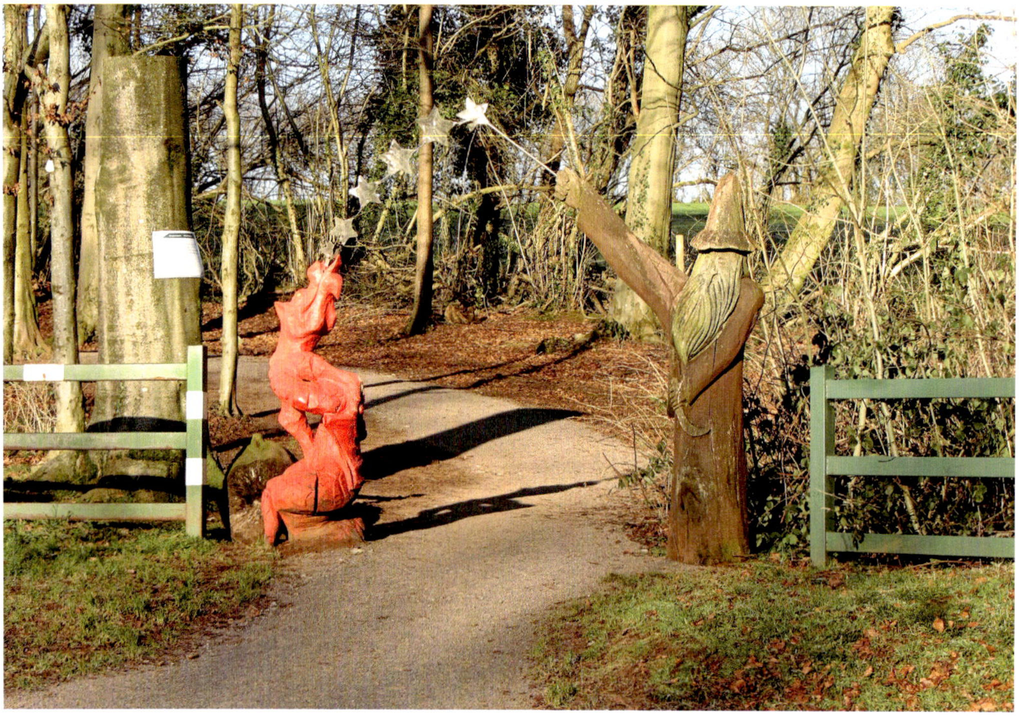

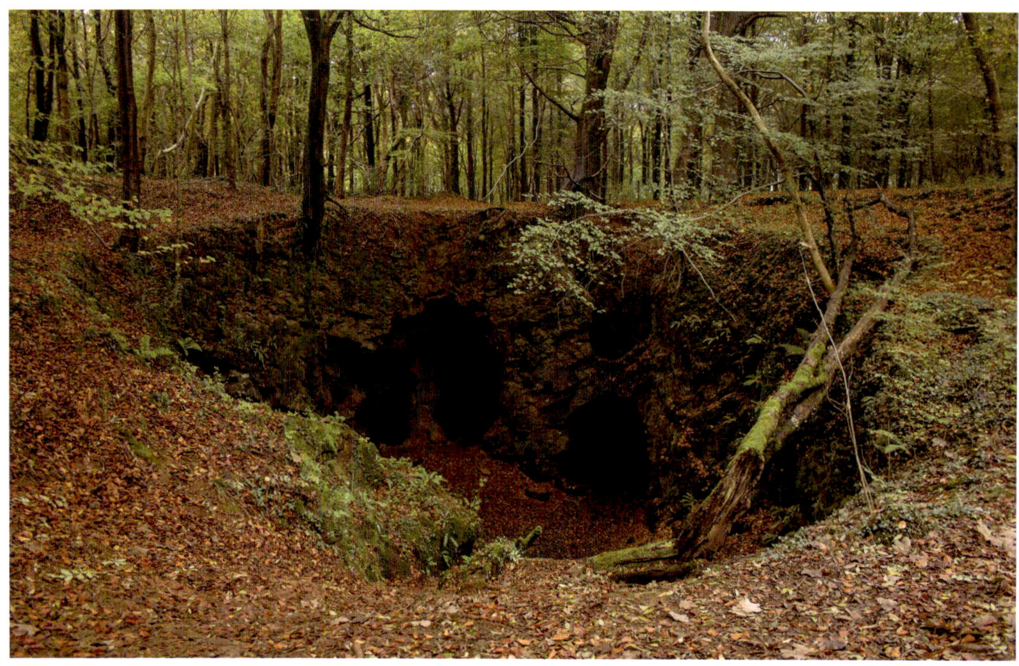

Sculpture trail entrance at Fforest Fawr. (© Gareth James (Wikimedia, CC BY-SA 2.0))

Three Bears Cave at Fforest Fawr. (© Jeremy Segrott (Wikimedia, CC BY 2.0))

Anyone hoping to see a dragon in Cardiff will find no shortage of them on the many patriotic flags dotting the city. For something a bit more life-sized, adventurous travellers might encounter a dragon on a fantastical trail that begins outside a fairy-tale castle. The Fforest Fawr Circular Walk starts at the Castell Coch car park in Tongwynlais, with alternative starting points available, and the different walks on offer range from a leisurely 1.1 miles to a longer 2.5 miles. The route features a sculpture trail designed to spark children's imaginations as they explore the ancient woodland, with carved characters inspired by the tales of *The Mabinogion* – including a potential fire-breathing monster – hidden among the trees.

Along the way, you'll discover evidence of Wales's industrial past, such as the evocatively named Three Bears Cave and the Blue Pool, a flooded limestone quarry pond, with remnants of old quarry workings nearby. Fairy tale enthusiasts can find even more magic within the walls of nearby Castell Coch, as we'll explore in the next entry.

Sleeping Beauty's Bedroom

Castell Coch is the fairy-tale castle of the third Marquess of Bute, a towering folly that peers over the ancient trees of Fforest Fawr and can be seen for miles around. Its name, meaning Red Castle in English, relates to the original red stones used in the creation of the castle, which began life in the thirteenth century on the site of an even earlier motte.

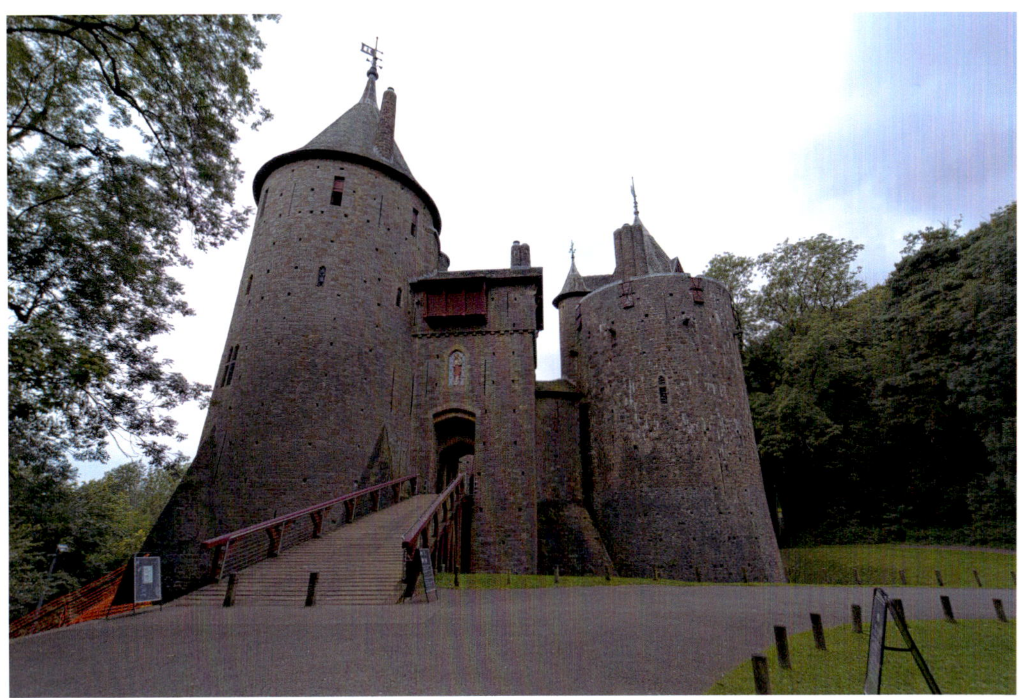

Castell Coch. (© Steve Collis (Flickr, CC BY 2.0))

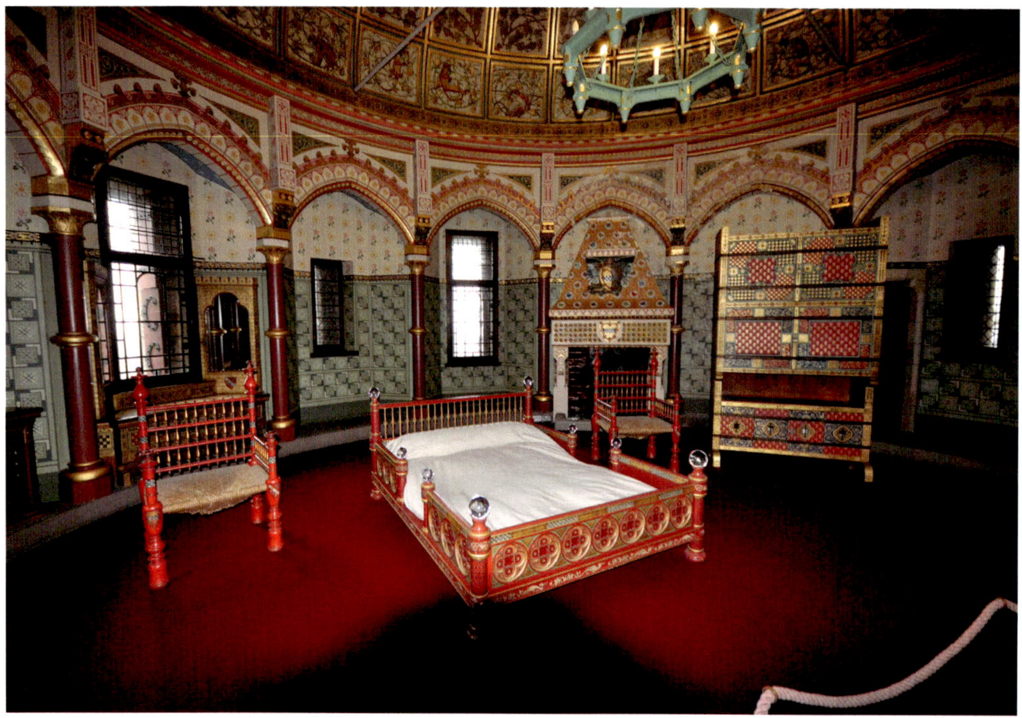

Lady Bute's bedroom. (© Nilfanion (Wikimedia, CC BY-SA 4.0))

It was on these ruins that Lord Bute gave his trusted architect, William Burges, permission to work his magic on the building, as he had previously done with Cardiff Castle. Burges embarked on the project full steam with his trademark enthusiasm for the Gothic Revival, so enamoured with Castell Coch that he even built a miniature version for himself in Kensington. He died in 1881, and his assistant William Frame, along with Bute and his wife, brought the work to completion. Much like Cardiff Castle, the decoration is heavy in symbolism and alludes to the designer and patron's passions for religion, travel, and literature, from the Virgin Mary that greets visitors as they enter the fortress to the Greek mythological figures depicted in the artwork.

Completed in 1891, the Butes' personal touches can be felt throughout, most notably in their private quarters. Bute's admiration of chivalrous knights might explain why his wife's bedroom is far more opulent than his own, a space rich in detail and finely decorated. With scenic views of the surrounding land, she occupied the room at the very top of the keep tower. What might not be apparent at first glance is that the bedroom is themed around a fairy tale. In fact, if you were lucky enough to spend the night there, you could take the starring role in *Sleeping Beauty*, but be warned: this is no Disney version of the story. While the castle itself has been compared to something that might be found in the 'magic kingdom', the theme was inspired by the grittier version of the tale as recorded by the Brothers Grimm. This is why anyone lying back in the bed, which has eight crystal balls attached to the frame, will gaze up at the highlight of the room – a golden dome on which animals can be seen among bramble scrolls and tangled foliage, a key element in the original story. The overall effect is topped off with mirrors that reflect the sparkling light from the chandelier, aiming to give the viewer a truly magical experience.

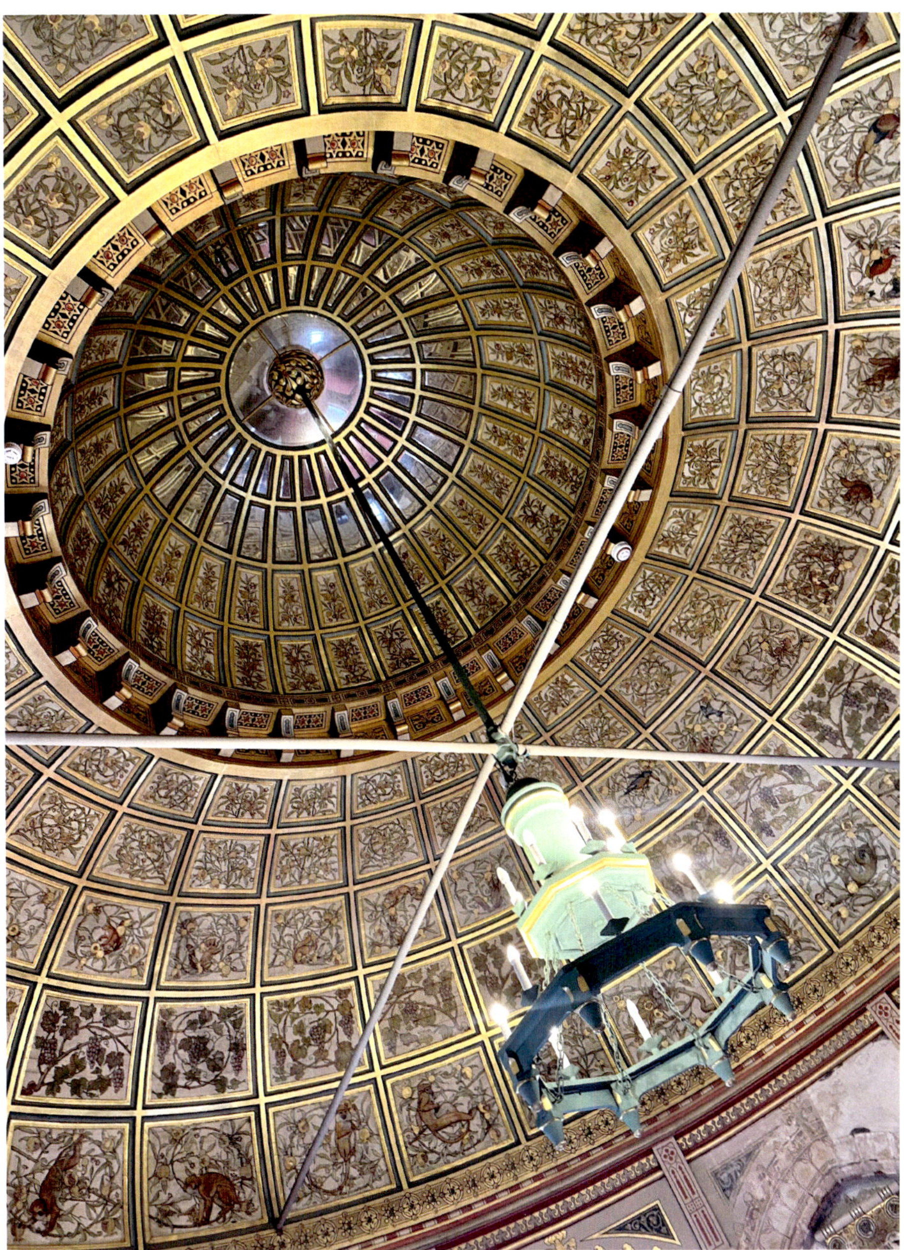

The ceiling above Lady Bute's bed. (© No Swan So Fine (Wikimedia, CC BY SA 4.0))

The Famous Cardiff Séance of 1919

In the archives of spiritualism, the 'famous Cardiff séance' of 15 February 1919 remains a standout event, captivating the public not only for the reported paranormal phenomena but also due to the high-profile attendees, including Sir Arthur Conan Doyle, the famed creator of Sherlock Holmes.

Hosted at the home of Mr Wall in Penylan, around twenty individuals gathered for an evening shrouded in mystery. The séance was led by the Thomas brothers, with Will Thomas as the medium and Tom Thomas as the master of ceremonies. The setting was a sparsely decorated first-floor room, where items for the main event were arranged, including a what-not stocked with various objects and an open bag containing a length of rope, a squeaking doll rattle, and a large tambourine.

The séance began with hymns, quickly transitioning into a mesmerising display of supposed ghostly activity. Will, the medium, spoke in an unfamiliar accent, attributing it to his spirit guide, White Eagle. Levitating items, such as the tambourine and rattle, moved around the room seemingly propelled by unseen forces. Instruments played, and a guitar slid about, rubbing against the participants' knees. The climax saw the what-not moving by itself and discarding objects around the room.

Astonishingly, the police were in attendance, and Chief Constable David Williams and his deputy had thoroughly examined the medium beforehand and tied him to a chair, finding no signs of trickery. Chief Constable Williams

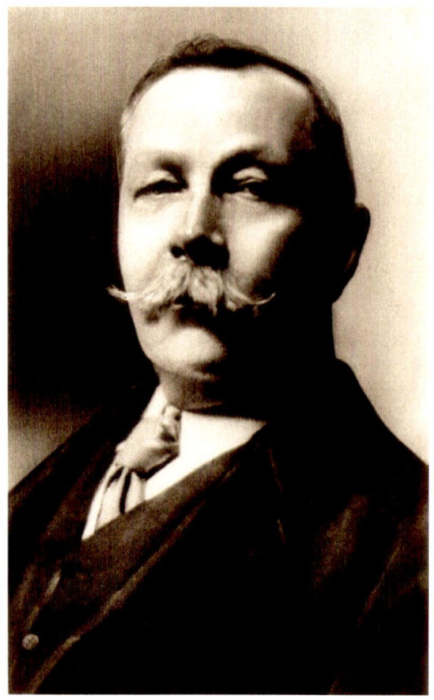

Sir Arthur Conan Doyle.

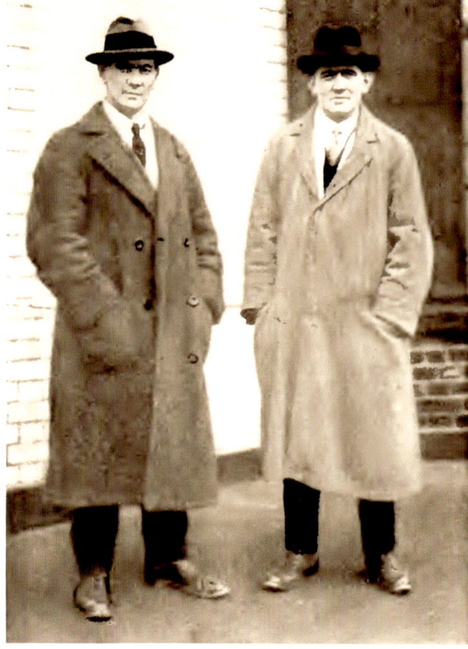

The Thomas Brothers.

described it as an 'interesting experience', although he admitted that, despite having an 'open mind,' he did not know how magicians created their illusions on the theatre stage either, therefore it was possible he could have been deceived.

As for Sir Arthur, he concluded that the events merely showcased the existence of 'intelligent powers' beyond ordinary senses, deeming the entire affair 'very elementary'. The 'famous Cardiff séance' left an indelible mark, a mystifying testament to the blurred boundaries between the natural and supernatural.

The Weird and Wonderful Water Tower

What was once a seemingly innocuous water tower just outside Cardiff Central station now stands as both a testament to the city's industrial history and its artistic vibrancy.

A landmark instantly recognisable to train commuters, it overlooks the River Taff near platform zero, where it was originally installed to supply water for the steam locomotives of the Great Western Railway. Standing 15 metres high, the Grade II listed building was completed in 1932, with its distinctive cylindrical tank supported by six sturdy concrete ribs and brick-filled panels adorning its exterior.

As the need for its original function waned, the tower evolved into a canvas for creative expression. Its exterior has been used for various purposes, from

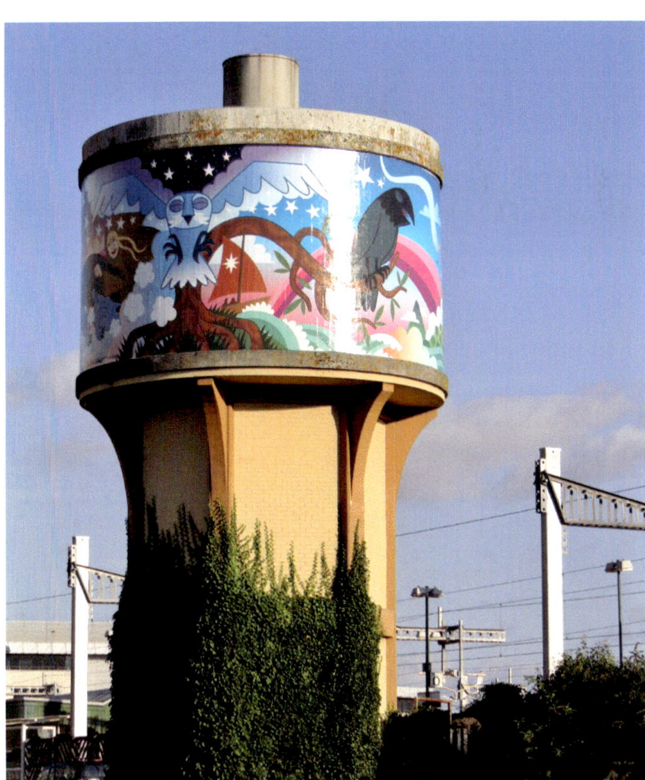

Water Tower at Cardiff Central station. (© Colin Smith (Wikimedia, CC BY-SA 2.0))

displaying sporting advertisements to eye-catching murals, such as a vibrant daffodil design in 1984.

Perhaps the most notable transformation occurred in April 2018, when a new mural inspired by Welsh mythology was revealed. Artist Pete Fowler, known for his instantly recognisable Super Furry Animals artwork, was commissioned to create a mural based on *The Mabinogion* as part of Literature Wales's Weird and Wonderful Wales project. The mural features legendary characters such as Bendigeidfran (Brân the Blessed), the giant king of Britain, and the flower maiden Blodeuwedd, adding a touch of medieval magic to the Cardiff skyline.

Pete the Poltergeist

In the 1980s, Cardiff became the scene of a headline-grabbing poltergeist mystery: the curious case of Pete the Poltergeist. It all began at Cardiff Mower Services, a lawnmower repair shop established in 1978 off Crwys Road, where stones were thrown at the roof of the workshop while the owner was working inside. The police could find no culprits, but the situation quickly escalated when objects started being thrown inside as well.

A séance conducted by shop owner John Matthews and his brother-in-law, Fred Cook, aimed to rule out human involvement – they reasoned that if they were all together around the workbench, they couldn't be responsible if any activity occurred. To their surprise, the activity continued and only served to convince them that the phenomenon was indeed paranormal in nature. The spirit responded to their requests by throwing stones and even engine parts, and a particularly 'active corner' of the premises was described as 'ice cold' and emitted a 'terrible smell of burning'.

They considered the 'poltergeist' to be a friendly presence, and affectionately named him Pete, viewing him as part of their extended family. Pete's mischief spread beyond the workshop, with neighbouring church officials also reporting stone-throwing incidents. Despite the occasional prank, Pete was perceived as more childlike than malicious, and some instances of his behaviour, such as setting out cutlery, suggested he was even trying to be helpful at times.

Nevertheless, they still wanted answers and enlisted the help of paranormal investigator David Fontana, a Professor of Psychology at Cardiff University and future president of the Society for Psychical Research (SPR). Fontana's meticulous investigation, lasting from 1989 to 1992, included unannounced visits and a thorough analysis of the phenomena. His findings revealed Pete's apparent intent and rudimentary intelligence, ruling out conventional explanations. Despite the possibility of an elaborate hoax, Fontana concluded that a definite intelligence was at play.

When Cardiff Mower Services relocated to a new premises, Pete bid them farewell. He did, however, allegedly continue to follow Cook, causing paranormal incidents at his home. When Cook broke a piece of pottery connected to Pete these incidents ceased, seemingly ending the spectral legacy of Pete the Poltergeist, a mysterious chapter in Cardiff's paranormal history.

Ianto's Shrine

If there's something strange in Cardiff Bay, who ya gonna call?

When BBC Wales revived the iconic sci-fi series *Doctor Who* in 2005, Cardiff became its central filming location. The show's success led to several spin-offs, including *Torchwood*, a covert organisation dedicated to investigating and combating extraterrestrial threats. The Torchwood Institute, led by Captain Jack Harkness (John Barrowman), undertook intergalactic missions, confronting various monsters and aliens from their base in Cardiff Bay.

One of the main characters, Ianto Jones, played by Gareth David-Lloyd, met his demise in 2009 during the show's third series. In response, a shrine dedicated to the fan favourite appeared on the boardwalk beneath the former 'tourist information office' used as the entrance to Torchwood Three at Mermaid Quay. Fans first laid flowers there in July 2009, immediately following Ianto's death in the 'Children of Earth' finale.

Though the show may have been off the air for many years, Ianto is gone but not forgotten. Ianto's Shrine has become a cultural landmark in Cardiff, with its own social media presence that attracts visitors from around the world. Whovians continue to contribute new items to the shrine, which is plastered with photographs, notes, poems, and trinkets. Superfans, such as Carol-Anne Hillman, ensure that the shrine is well maintained and updated.

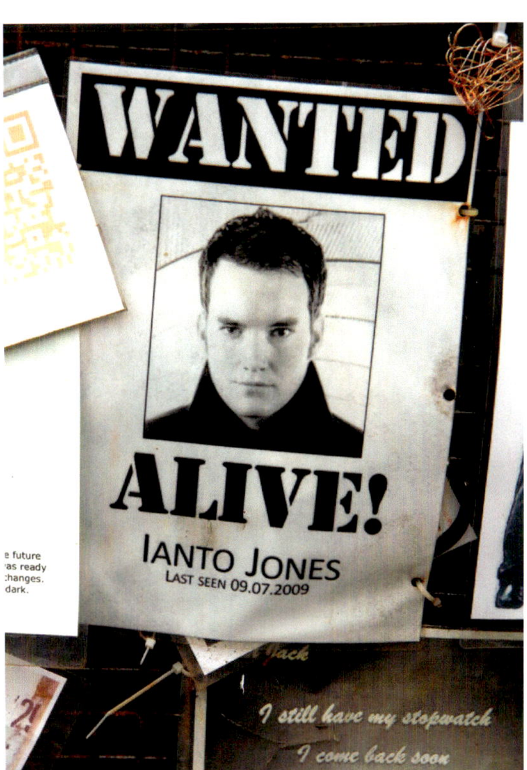

A poster of Ianto Jones (Gareth David-Lloyd) at Ianto's Shrine. (© Richard Croft (Wikimedia, CC BY-SA 2.0 DEED))

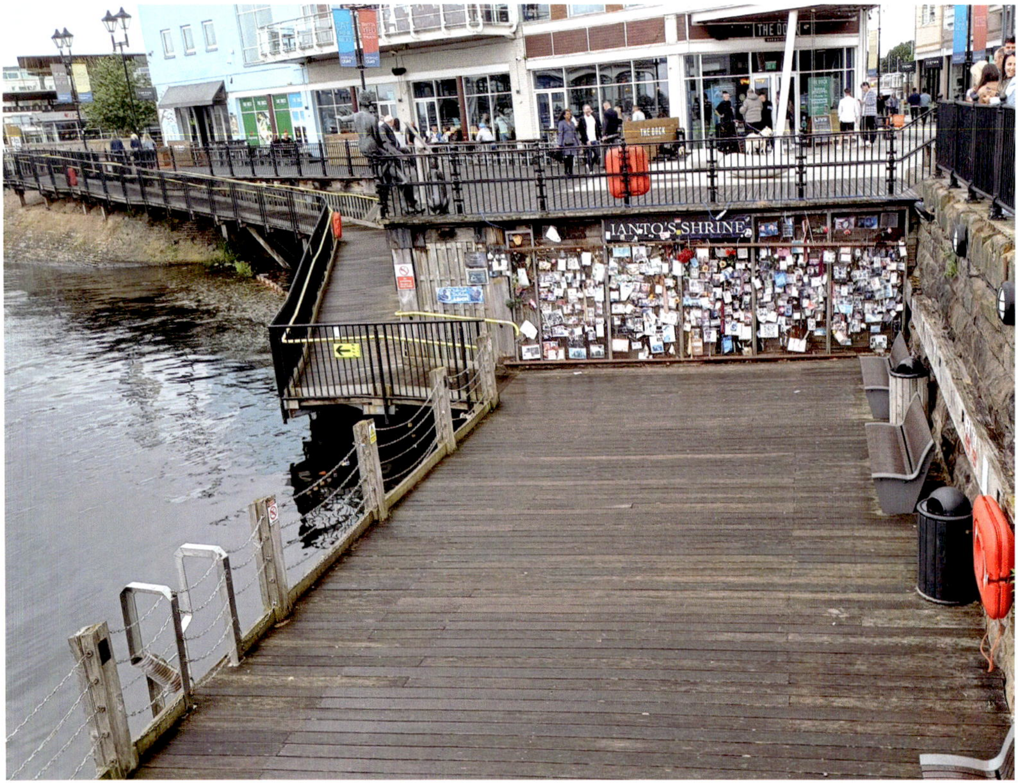

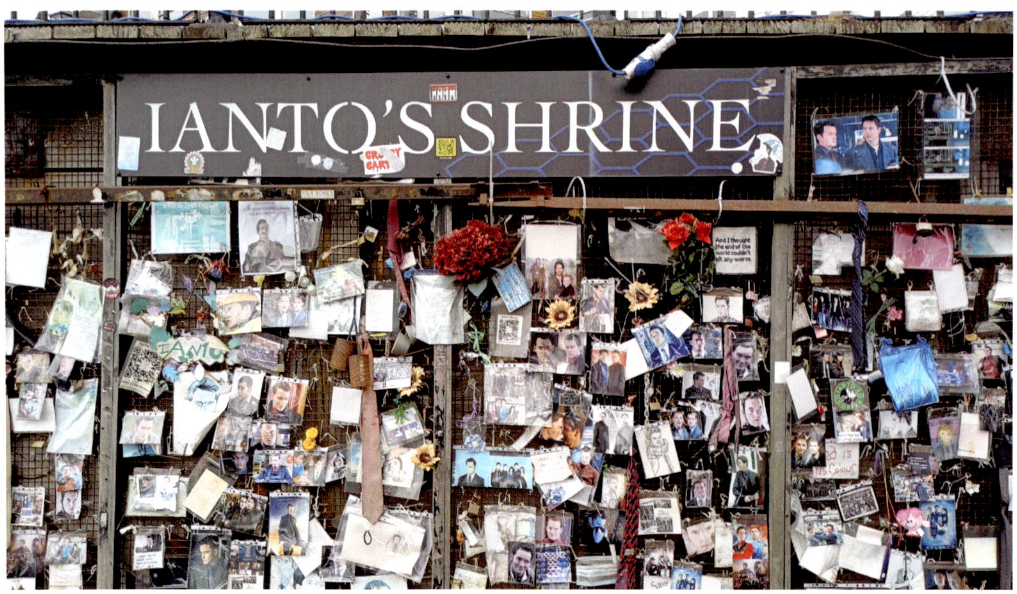

Approaching Ianto's Shrine.

Close-up of Ianto's Shrine.

Sport and Nightlife

Cardiff is the beating heart of Wales, and two things often combine to attract visitors to the city centre each year: sport and nightlife.

A rich sporting heritage has flowed through the city's veins for centuries, with fervent cheers echoing from historic venues like the Arms Park and Ninian Park to more recent additions such as the Principality Stadium and Cardiff City Stadium. Whether it's watching Wales in the Six Nations or the Bluebirds in league action, Cardiff's deep-rooted passion for sport is a hallmark of the city, permeating every aspect of its identity. As such, these sporting arenas have become hallowed grounds where dreams are forged and legacies are born.

When the match is over, the city's nightlife offers a different kind of allure. Conveniently within walking distance of the major sporting venues, you'll find everything from quaint pubs off the beaten track to the hottest clubs pulsating with energy. The same passion that fuels the terraces is carried over into a night out on the town.

In this final chapter, we explore some unique aspects of Cardiff's sporting and nightlife heritage, from shared triumphs and forgotten heroes to the unforgettable memories made in the city's more colourful bars, clubs, and hotels.

Gwyn Nicholls Memorial Gates

The Gwyn Nicholls Memorial Gates, unveiled on Boxing Day in 1949 at Cardiff Arms Park, serve as a poignant tribute to one of Wales's rugby legends. Gwyn Nicholls, born in Gloucestershire on 15 July 1874, left an indelible mark on rugby history as the 'Prince of Threequarters'. His illustrious career included twenty-four caps for Wales as a centre, establishing him as one of the most formidable players of his era.

Nicholls kicked off his rugby career in Cardiff in 1891, making his first-team debut in 1893. Except for a brief stint with Newport in the 1901–02 season, he remained with the club until 1906, captaining the team for four seasons and significantly influencing their achievements both on and off the pitch. Internationally, he debuted against Scotland in 1896 and swiftly became a standout player. He captained Wales in ten matches, notably returning from retirement in 1905 to lead the team in the historic 'Match of the Century' – more on that in the next entry.

Following his retirement, tragedy struck in 1923 when Nicholls attempted a daring rescue of two girls swept out to sea at Weston-super-Mare. Although the girls were saved by another brave man, his health suffered as a result, leading to

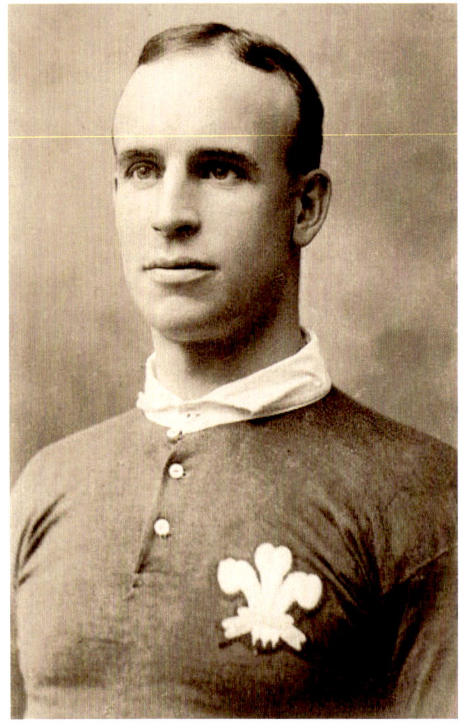

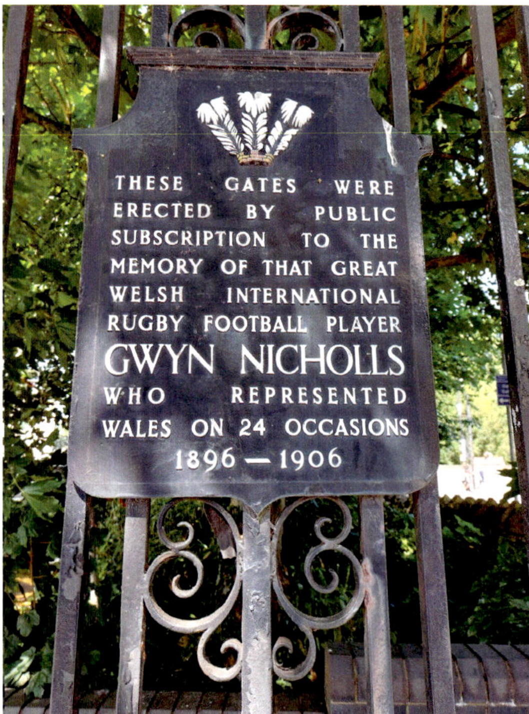

Above left: Gwyn Nicholls (1874–1939).

Above right: The Gwyn Nicholls Memorial Gates at Cardiff Arms Park. (Photo by Emma Hardy)

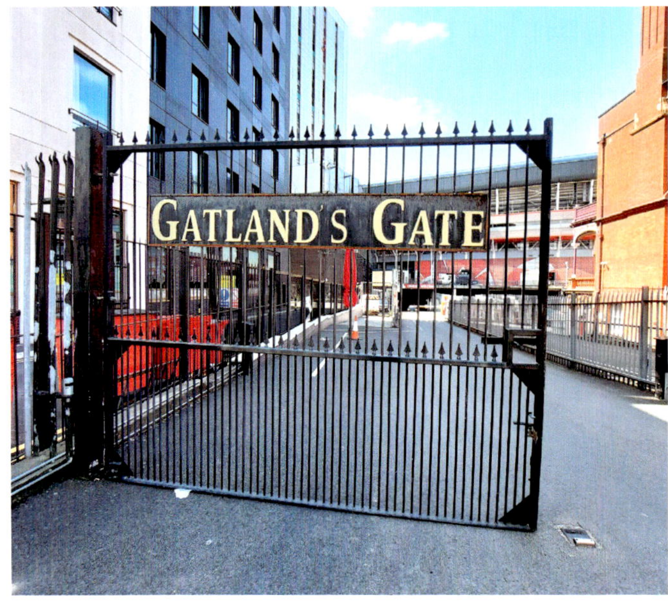

Gatland's Gate at the Principality Stadium. (Photo by Emma Hardy)

his passing on 24 March 1939 due to heart failure. The Gwyn Nicholls Memorial Gates stand as a testament to his enduring impact on Welsh rugby, and he was posthumously inducted into the International Rugby Hall of Fame in 2005, solidifying his place among rugby's greats.

In more recent times, another hero of Welsh rugby was also honoured with gates named after him. The Welsh Rugby Union (WRU) renamed Gate 4 of the Principality Stadium as Gatland's Gate in honour of Warren Gatland, 'arguably the most successful coach in its history'.

Match of the Century

When Wales squared up against New Zealand at Cardiff Arms Park on 16 December 1905, little did they know that more than 100 years later it would be described as the 'Match of the Century', and not just for the scoreline. Drawing a crowd of 47,000, this clash of the top two international teams also marked the historic moment that a national anthem was sung before an international sporting event for the first time.

Before arriving in Wales, the All Blacks had dominated the game, not conceding a single point in their last 600 minutes of rugby. Wales themselves boasted an undefeated record in 1905 and anticipation ran high; the atmosphere surrounding the game was electrifying. Extra trains were arranged for the influx

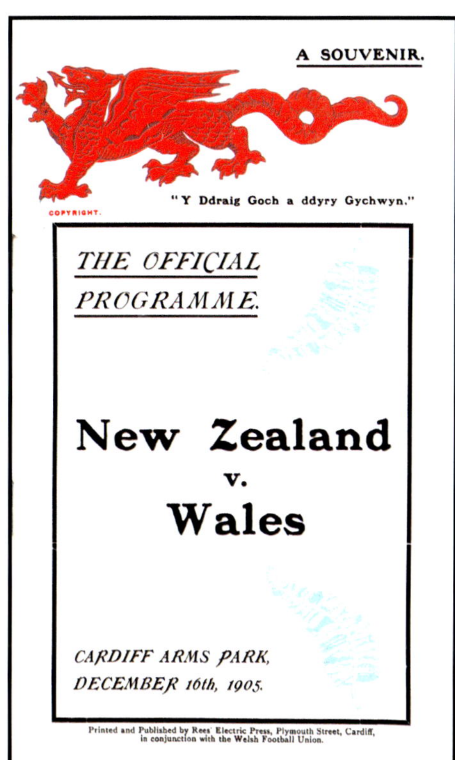

The official programme for New Zealand v Wales at Cardiff Arms Park on 16 December 1905.

of spectators to Cardiff, and by 1.30 p.m., the gates had to be shut as the ground reached full capacity. Before the game began, New Zealand performed their traditional haka, a ceremonial Māori war dance meant to fire up the team and intimidate their opponents. Immediately in response, the Welsh players, led by Teddy Morgan, began singing 'Hen Wlad Fy Nhadau' ('Land of My Fathers'), which was soon being belted out by the entire crowd. This symbolic moment is seen as marking the first recorded instance of a national anthem being sung before an international sporting fixture.

On the field, Wales, with innovative scrummaging tactics, held their ground against the formidable All Blacks. Despite New Zealand's improved performance in the second half, Wales secured the victory with the match's only try, scored by the anthem-starter Morgan. The final score was 3-0 and the aftermath saw the crowd wildly celebrating the Welsh triumph, carrying the players on their shoulders. Despite disputes over the result, New Zealand's captain, Dave Gallaher, conceded that 'the best team won'. Referring to the anthem singing, he said: 'Imagine some 40,000 people singing their national anthem with all the fervour of which the Celtic heart is capable. It was the most impressive incident I have ever witnessed on a football field.'

The centenary celebrations in 2005 saw the two teams square off in Cardiff once more. Despite an impressive attendance of 74,402 at the Millennium Stadium, the passionate Welsh fans singing the national anthem couldn't stop the All Blacks from cruising to a crushing 41-3 victory, with 26 points scored by Dan Carter. The only points scored by Wales came from a Stephen Jones penalty kick.

The Stadium's Cursed Room

The Millennium Stadium, now the Principality Stadium, has been a venue of notable firsts. It was the first stadium to host an indoor rugby match under a fully retractable roof, and the first stadium to host the FA Cup final outside of England. Yet there is one first nobody could have foreseen: it was, presumably, the first stadium in the world to require an exorcist to cleanse a 'cursed' changing room.

Teams assigned to the 'room of doom', as the south changing room became ominously known, before major matches consistently faced defeat. With Wembley Stadium closed for renovations, the curse ensnared some of sport's most formidable contenders, and even football giants like Arsenal, Tottenham, and Chelsea – equipped with their supposed 'lucky' white socks – succumbed to it.

An unconventional solution was found in the form of Andrew Vicari, the Port Talbot-born artist hailed as 'Britain's richest living painter'. He offered his services to paint a colourful scene that might dismiss any bad vibes in the room, acting as an artist-cum-exorcist. Stadium management were happy to give it a go, and he crafted a vibrant 7-foot mural of fiery reds, oranges, and yellows that depicted a blazing sun rising behind a galloping horse and a soaring phoenix.

Stoke City became the litmus test for Vicari's artistic intervention during the 2002 Division Two play-off final against Brentford. The odds were staggering,

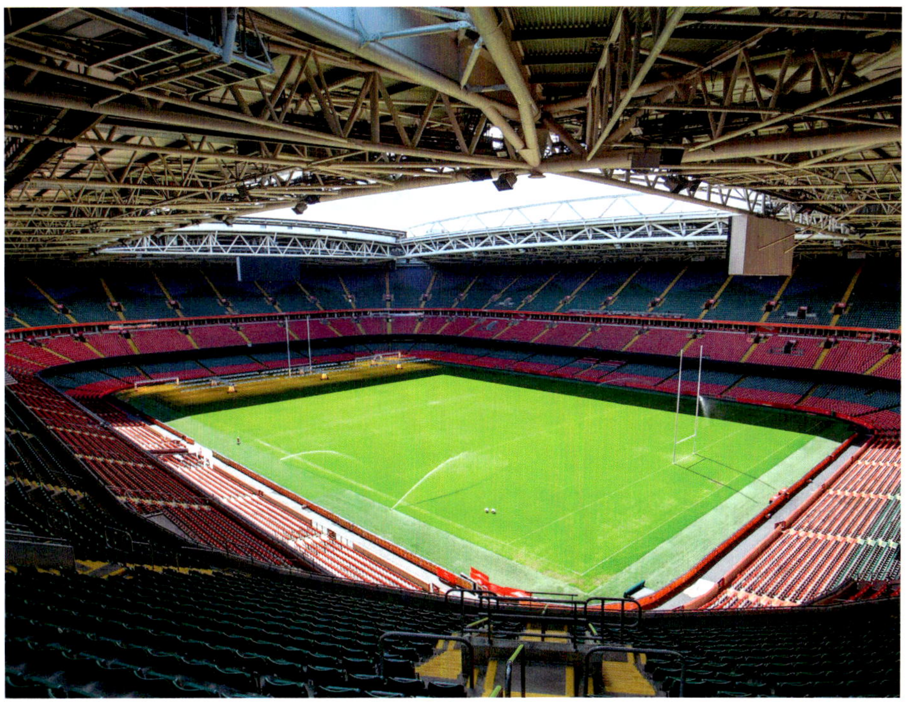

Principality Stadium. (© Visit Wales (CC BY-SA 4.0))

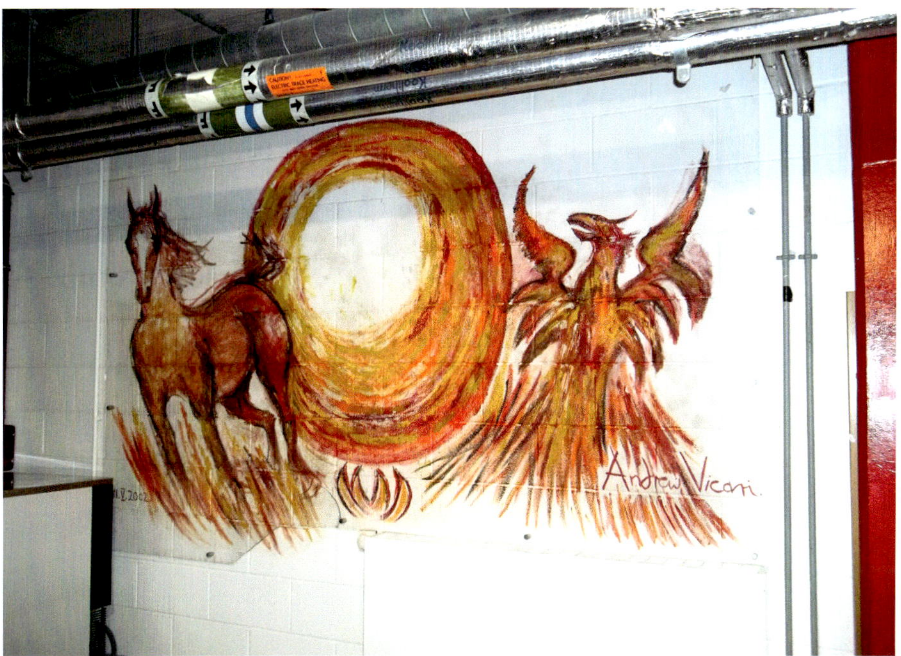

Andrew Vicari's mural. (© Mark Healey (Flickr, CC BY-SA 2.0))

with eleven consecutive losses for teams in the room amounting to roughly 8,000/1, according to the *Stoke Sentinel*. Nevertheless, Stoke shattered the curse and emerged victorious with a 2-0 win.

Speaking pragmatically to the BBC, the stadium's chairman expressed delight at the curse's end, likening it to the inevitable conclusion of tossing a coin – 'it had to end sometime'. Vicari's vibrant artwork not only added a touch of colour to the stadium, and a unique chapter to its history, but also seemingly dispelled the spectre of the cursed changing room – or was it all just a coincidence?

The Rugby Codebreakers

Rugby is, symbolically at least, the unofficial sport of Wales. More specifically, rugby union is the unofficial sport of Wales, and rugby league, while it has its passionate fanbase, is more of a niche sport on Welsh soil when compared to its heartland in the north of England.

Despite this, 'three of the greatest rugby players in the history of the game' were born in Cardiff and were commemorated in a statue for their remarkable contributions to rugby league in 2023. Two of these legends, Billy Boston, born on 6 August 1934 in Butetown, and Clive Sullivan, born on 9 April 1943 in Splott, have the distinction of being the first non-fictionalised black men to be honoured with statues in Wales. The statue, commissioned as part of the community-led 'One Team. One Race' project in 2020, also honours Gus Risman, born on 21

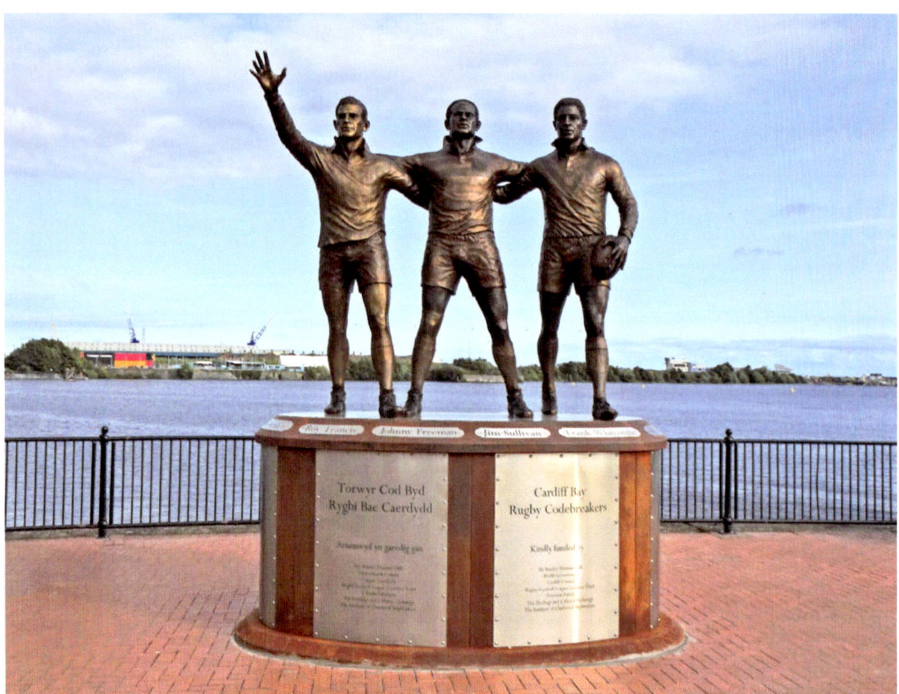

Statue of the Cardiff Bay Rugby Codebreakers. (© Sionk (Wikimedia, CC BY-SA 4.0))

March 1911. These three players, known as the 'codebreakers', were part of a group of thirteen athletes from in and around Cardiff Bay who excelled in rugby league. Their achievements include three Rugby League Hall of Famers and four members of the Welsh Sports Hall of Fame.

At the unveiling of the statue, Welsh rugby union legend Sir Gareth Edwards told ITV News that 'they were some of my heroes'. He added, 'It is recognition of some local heroes who have been neglected possibly, for want of a better word, due to the fact that they played rugby league which was frowned upon in this part of the world back in those days, in my early career.' Edwards himself is immortalised in Cardiff, with a bronze statue created by sculptor Bonar Dunlop in 1982, depicting him in a familiar pose, ready to throw the ball from his plinth, at the centre of St Davids Shopping Centre.

The Unmarked Grave of Cardiff City's Founder

It would be quite easy to fill a book of this size with fascinating facts about Cardiff City FC. For example, the Bluebirds were the first non-English club to win the FA Cup in 1927. Record goal scorer Len Davies found the net 181 times in league and cup games between 1920 and 1931. The quickest goal in club history was scored on 23 October 1954 by Trevor Ford, who netted against Charlton Athletic at the Valley in just fifteen seconds.

A less well-known fact is that the legendary club founder Bartley Wilson (3 January 1870–19 November 1954) was far from your typical Welsh sports fan; in fact, he was a disabled artist from England. Also, he didn't start the club for footballers; rather, it was created for cricketers. Perhaps most unexpected of all is that when this celebrated figure passed away, his final resting place was left unmarked for forty-five years.

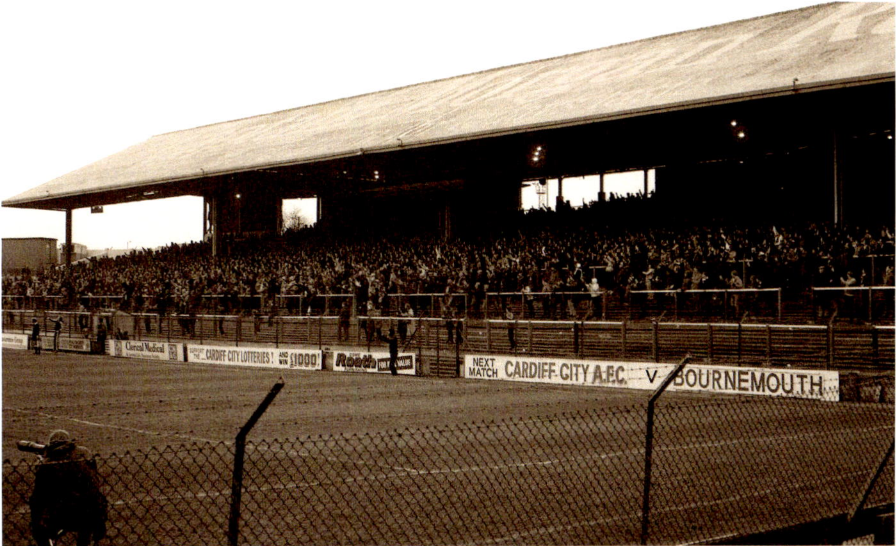

The bank terrace at Ninian Park in 1983. (© Steve Daniels (Wikimedia, CC BY-SA 2.0))

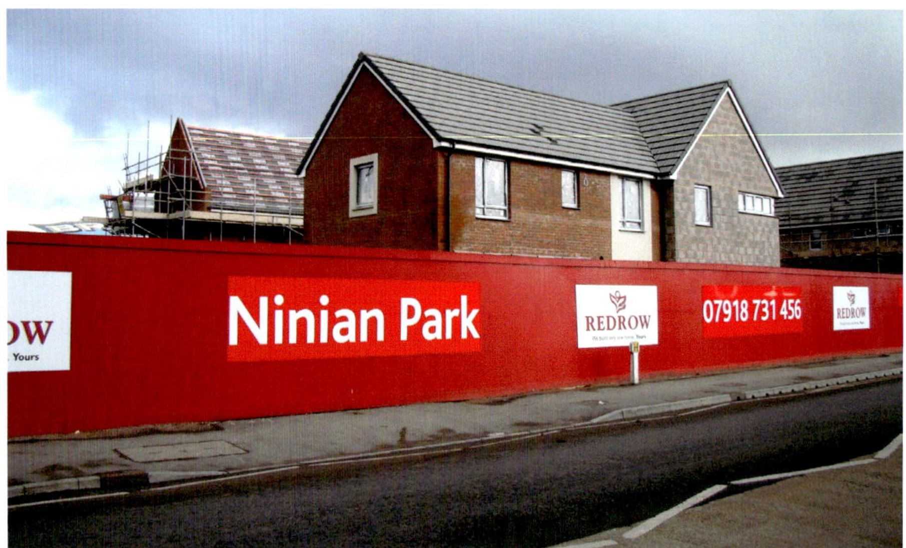

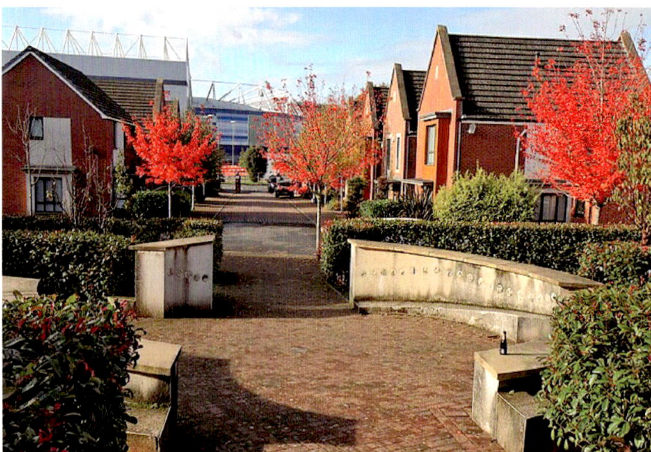

Above: Constructing new houses on the site of Ninian Park in 2010. (© Jon Candy (Flickr, CC BY-SA 2.0))

Left: The garden and artwork that marks the centre spot of Ninian Park in Bartley Wilson Way. (© Sionk (Wikimedia, CC BY-SA 4.0))

Born in Bristol, Wilson moved to Cardiff in his late twenties and joined Riverside Cricket Club, where he introduced a novel idea. A sport called 'soccer' was gaining popularity back in his hometown, and as it was played during the winter months when there was no cricket, starting a team would be a great excuse for the members to continue meeting during the darker part of the year. While interest was initially low, with barely enough attendees to field a five-a-side team, it gained momentum, and in 1899 Riverside AFC was formed. Their first game was against Barry West End on 7 October 1899, with Wilson as secretary.

Juggling his responsibilities with his day job at a local printer, the lithographic artist worked tirelessly to grow the club. A newspaper columnist writing in 1903 noted how the football club was 'rapidly coming to the front', and while it was a team game that required everyone pulling together, there was one man to be thanked in particular: 'none is the credit of this due more than Mr Bartley Wilson'. They also acknowledged how Wilson, being a humble man who worked quietly without blowing his own trumpet, would hate such public praise, but they were willing to risk his wrath to give him his due.

When Cardiff was named a city in 1905, Wilson began the process of having the name of the team changed to suit. In 1910, he oversaw the switch to a professional club and played a crucial role in securing Ninian Park as their home. When this historical ground closed its doors a century later in 2010, a housing estate was built on the site, where a road was named in his honour: Bartley Wilson Way. Wilson even had a short stint as manager in 1933.

In 1954, Wilson died at his home in Llanfair Road, Canton. He is buried alongside his wife in Western Cemetery, Ely. His funeral, however, which was attended by players past and present, was postponed by a day due to torrential rain. In the confusion, his headstone was placed under a nearby tree, and following the delay, was knocked over and seemingly lost. Remarkably, it was concealed in the undergrowth, and there it remained until it was rediscovered in 1998. It now stands proudly in its proper place in memory of the man who founded the Bluebirds.

The Vulcan Hotel

The Vulcan Hotel is a historic pub that once stood at No. 10 Adam Street in Adamsdown, or Newtown as it was known then. It now serves drinks in a different part of Cardiff, having been carefully relocated to its new home in St Fagans National Museum of History.

Newtown was a once-thriving community that sprang up in the Victorian age to provide housing for those working in the docklands area. Dubbed 'Little Ireland' due to the predominantly Irish population who had crossed the Irish Sea to escape the famine, it was here that the Vulcan was created by knocking two adjoining terraced houses into one. First opening its doors in 1853 as the Vulcan Inn, it also offered rooms to lodgers. After a significant facelift, it was renamed the Vulcan Hotel in 1915. Drastically remodelled, the building was extended upwards and given a new façade that resembles the building we see today. The drinking spaces inside reflected the culture of the time, with the main bar being a men-only area with no seats and sawdust on the floor, while the Smoke Room was more welcoming to couples.

In later years, the Vulcan became the watering hole of choice for many musicians, actors, and wordsmiths, several of whom came to its defence when it was under threat of demolition. Speaking in 2011, James Dean Bradfield from the Manic Street Preachers told *The Guardian* that it was his favourite Cardiff pub and bemoaned the fact that so many traditional Welsh pubs had been transformed beyond recognition. Somewhat prophetically, he claimed: 'Progress would change everything that I love about somewhere like the Vulcan, somewhere that seems to seep history through the very walls.' Fortunately, those walls were carefully deconstructed after the pub closed in May 2012, rebuilt at St Fagans, and reopened on 11 May 2024 as a working pub within the museum's collection.

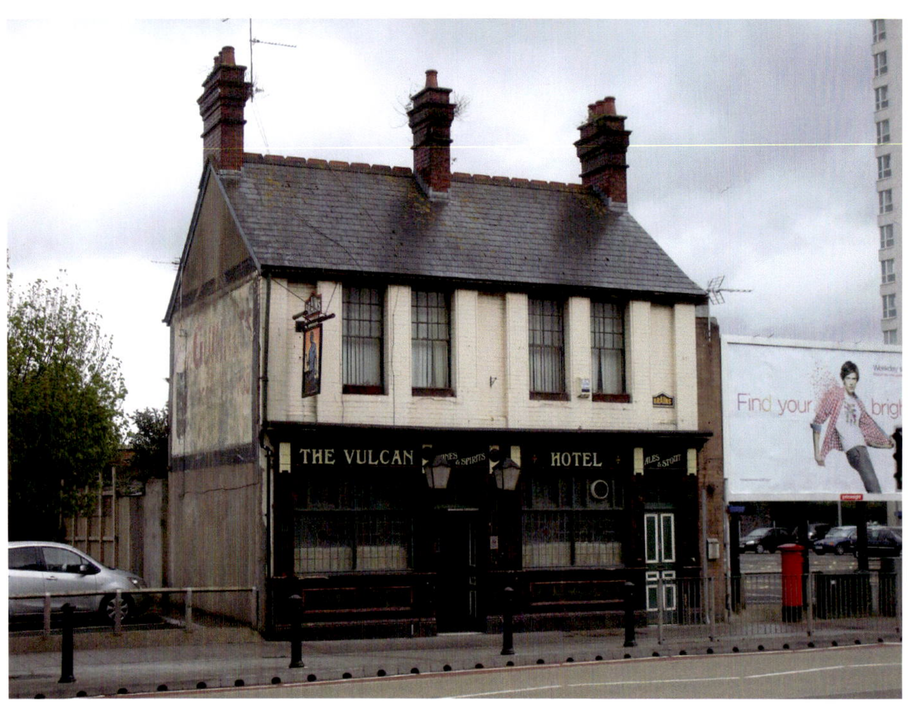

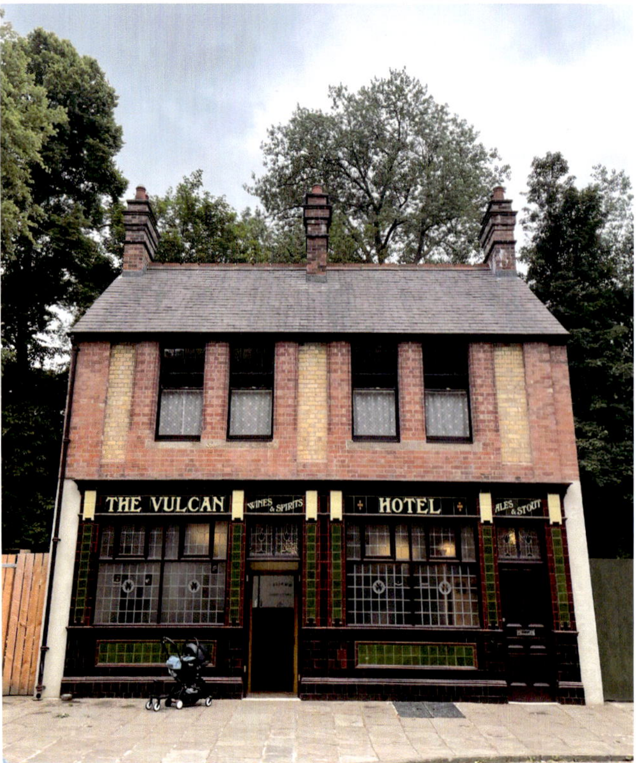

Above: The Vulcan Hotel in its original location on Adam Street in 2010. (© John Lord (Wikimedia, CC BY-SA 2.0))

Left: The Vulcan Hotel reconstructed at St Fagans National Museum of History. (© Llemiles (Wikimedia, CC0 1.0))

The Prince of Wales

If there's one pub guaranteed to be bustling on an international day, it's the Prince of Wales on St Mary Street. A short walk from both the stadium and the train station, with a main entrance on Wood Street, it's ideally located for fans to stop off at before and after the match. But drinkers popping into the Wetherspoons for a pint or two might have noticed that, for a drinking establishment, it has a rather regal appearance. In fact, both the exterior and interior hint at the building's former lives, and a close look will reveal clues to its original use.

The Grade II listed building opened on 7 October 1878 as the New Theatre Royal. The handiwork of architects WD Blessley and T Waring, its grand Venetian Gothic façade reflected Cardiff's booming Victorian economy. At the time of opening, it had the capacity to seat nearly 2,000 theatregoers, and such was its success, showing performances even after dark by gaslight, that this was increased to nearly 3,000. Changing with the times, in the early 1900s it was given a Greek makeover and the addition of the St Mary's Street entrance, with its distinctive frieze of a Grecian female standing between two Doric columns.

The twentieth century saw mixed fortunes for the building. During periods of closure and reinvention, it had stints as The Playhouse and The Prince of Wales theatre, from which the current name was taken, and as Caesar's Nightclub. There

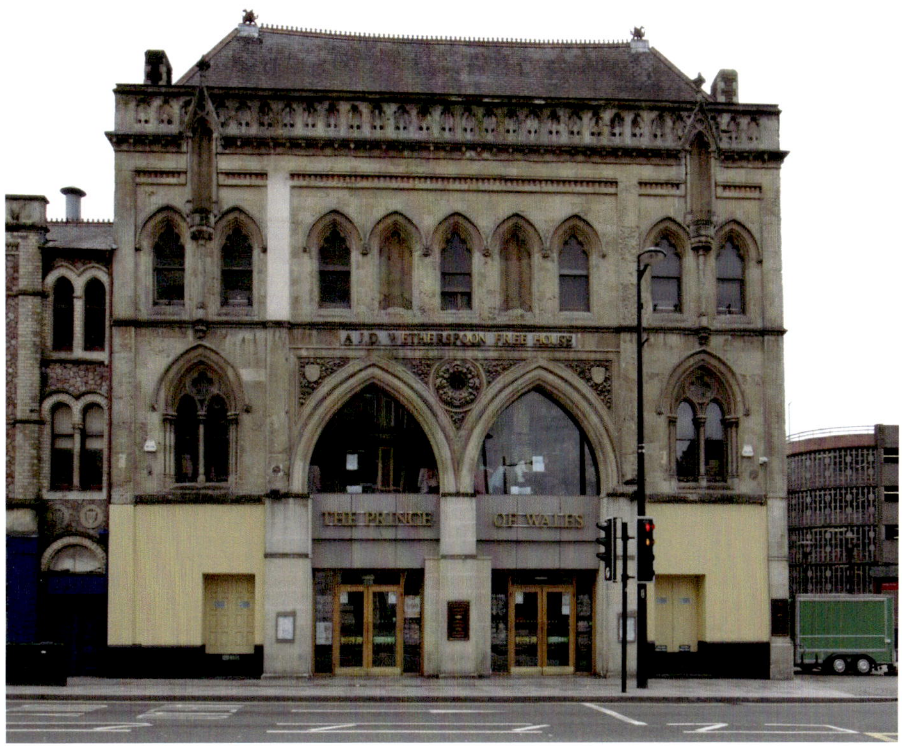

The Prince of Wales. (© Verbcatcher (Wikimedia, CC BY-SA 4.0))

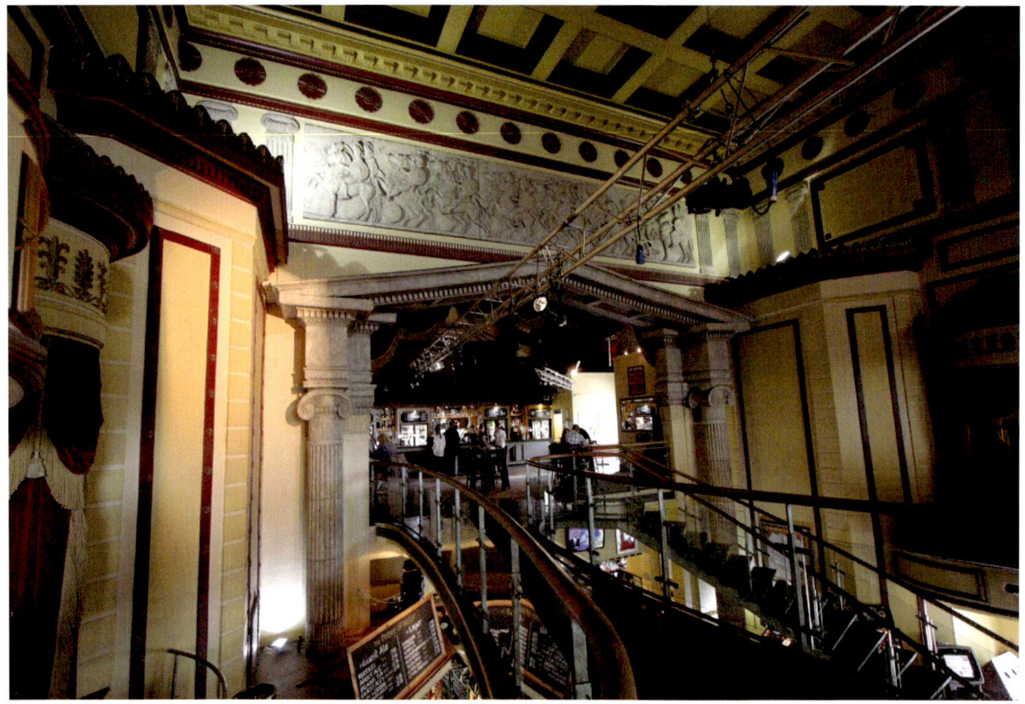

Interior of the Prince of Wales. (© Verbcatcher (Wikimedia, CC BY-SA 4.0))

was also an infamous period between the 1960s and 1970s when it specialised in films of an adult nature. In 1999, it was transformed into its current incarnation as a pub by Wetherspoons. During this restoration, some of its original features were revealed once more, offering punters a unique glimpse into Cardiff's past as they sip their drinks.

Chippy Lane

Finally, the only way to end this book, as with any good night out in Cardiff, is by taking a stroll down Caroline Street or, as it's better known, Chippy Lane or Chip Alley – two delectable nicknames that stand as testament to its culinary significance.

Tucked between the Hayes and St Mary's Street in the centre of town, this vibrant pedestrianised street boasts a rich history and architectural charm alongside its reputation with fast-food enthusiasts, where food can be 'cheap as chips' and perfect for rounding off an evening out.

Long before it became a go-to foodie destination, the street was originally part of Cardiff's town walls and situated south of the historic gaol. Renamed in the Victorian era after Caroline of Brunswick, the former Princess of Wales and wife of the future King George IV, it housed a mixture of trades, including bird dealers, butchers, cobblers, and watchmakers. There were also drinking establishments in

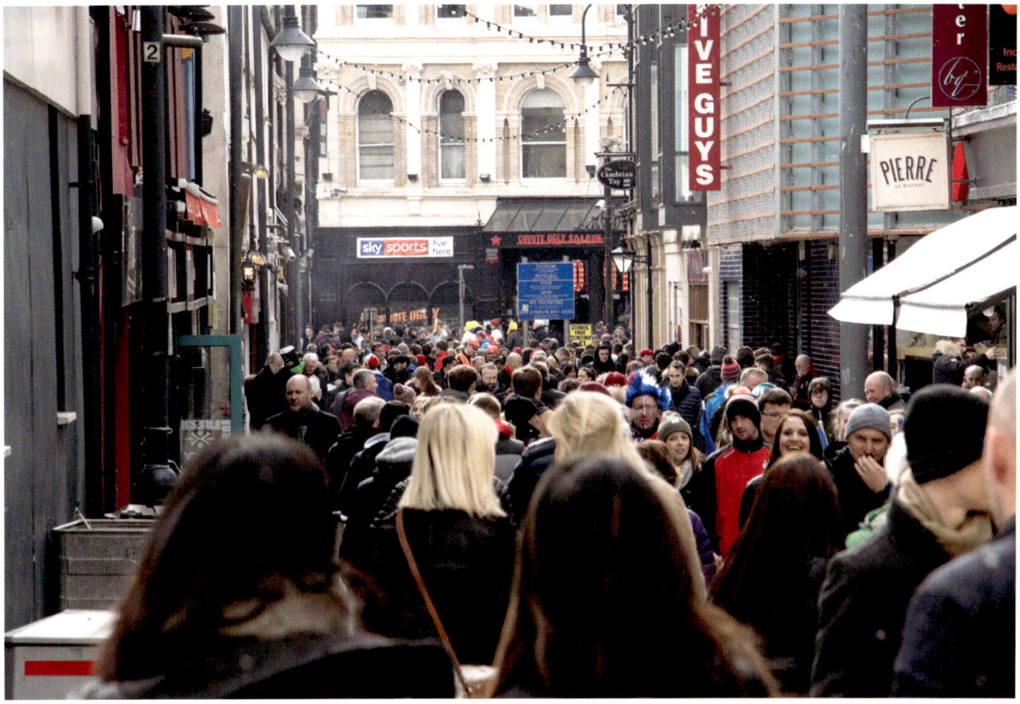

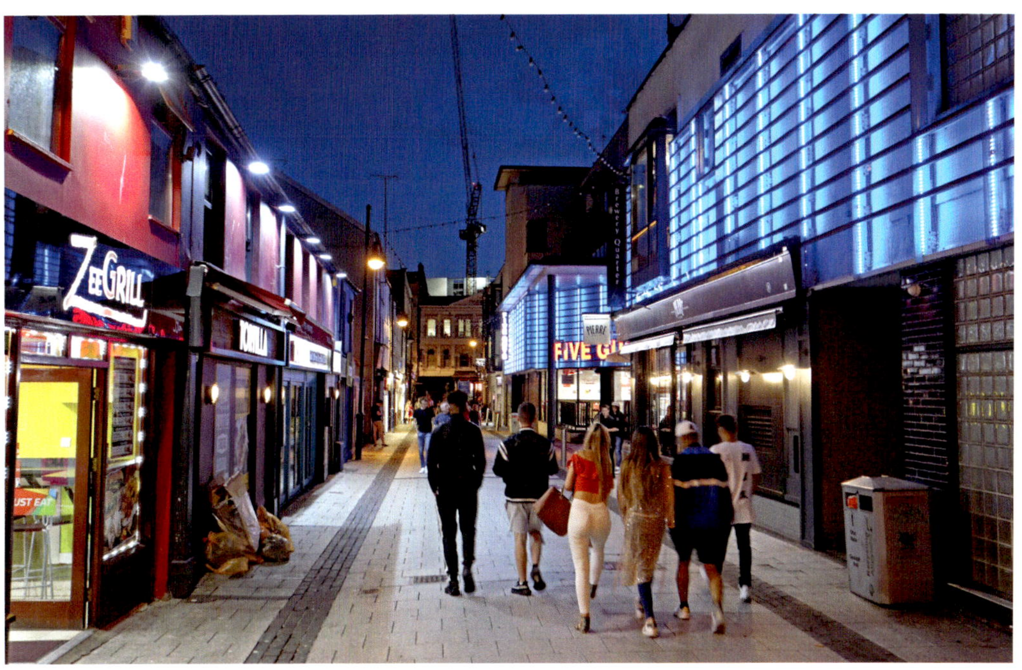

Caroline Street on match day during the Six Nations. (© Jeremy Segrott (Flickr, CC BY 2.0))

Night-time on Caroline Street. (© Allie_Caulfield (Flickr, CC BY 2.0))

the early days like the Kings Cross, which opened in 1872 and became known as 'Wales's oldest gay pub'.

Following the Second World War, Caroline Street began its transformation into a haven for family-owned food establishments. Dorothy's Cafe & Fish Bar, established in 1953, proudly claims to be the oldest fast-food shop on the street. Adding to the street's appeal are the late opening hours, with some restaurants serving until 2 a.m. on busier nights. Although antisocial behaviour can occasionally be an issue, and leftover food an unsightly problem the next morning, the lively atmosphere has made the street a beloved part of Cardiff's lore. It has even entered the realm of pop culture, being name-dropped by Nessa (Ruth Jones) in the hit BBC sitcom *Gavin & Stacey* – tidy!

Bibliography

Cannon, John, and Crowcroft, Robert, *A Dictionary of British History 3 ed.* (Oxford University Press, 2015)

Davies, John, *Broadcast and the BBC in Wales* (University of Wales Press, 1994)

Davies, J., Jenkins, N., Baines, M., and Lynch, P. I., *The Welsh Academy Encyclopaedia of Wales* (University of Wales Press, 2008)

Fawkes, Richard, *Welsh National Opera* (Julia MacRae, 1986)

Lord, Peter, *Imaging the Nation* (University of Wales Press, 2004)

Owen, Trefor M., *Welsh Folk Customs* (Gomer, 1994)

Rees, Mark, *Ghosts of Wales: Accounts from the Victorian Archives* (The History Press, 2017)

Rees, Mark, *Paranormal Wales* (Amberley Publishing, 2020)

Sikes, Wirt, *British Goblins* (EP Publishing Limited, 1973)

Waite, Maurice, *Oxford Paperback Thesaurus* (Oxford University Press, 2012)

Online resources

bbc.co.uk
captainscottsociety.com
cardiffcastle.com
gov.uk
guardian.com
itv.com
llandaffcathedral.org.uk
museum.wales
outdoorcardiff.com
royalhotelcardiff.com
senedd.wales
visitwales.com
walesonline.com
wru.wales

Acknowledgements

A huge *diolch o galon* to my family for their continued support, and to Nick Grant and all at Amberley Publishing for commissioning the book you now hold in your hands. *Quirky Cardiff* was made possible thanks to the fantastic work and research of those who trod a similar path to myself in centuries gone by who have been mentioned throughout and/or referenced in the bibliography, and the photographers whose fantastic images have been credited throughout.

About the Author

For more than two decades, Mark Rees has published articles about the arts in some of Wales's bestselling newspapers and magazines. His roles have included arts editor for the *South Wales Evening Post*, *Carmarthen Journal*, *Llanelli Star* and *Swansea Life*, with work appearing in the *Western Mail*, *WalesOnline*, *South Wales Echo* and *Glamorgan Gazette*. He has written a number of books, with those of a 'quirky' nature including *Ghosts of Wales: Accounts from the Victorian Archives* (2017), *The A–Z of Curious Wales* (2019), *Paranormal Wales* (2020), *Paranormal Cardiff* (2023), and *Paranormal Swansea and Gower* (2024). In 2017 he launched the now-annual 'Ghosts of Wales – Live!' Halloween event, and in 2018 *Phantoms*, a play based on his ghost stories, was adapted for the stage by Fluellen Theatre Group. Rees has spoken widely on the paranormal and folklore for major broadcasters including the BBC, international podcasts, and at conferences across the UK.

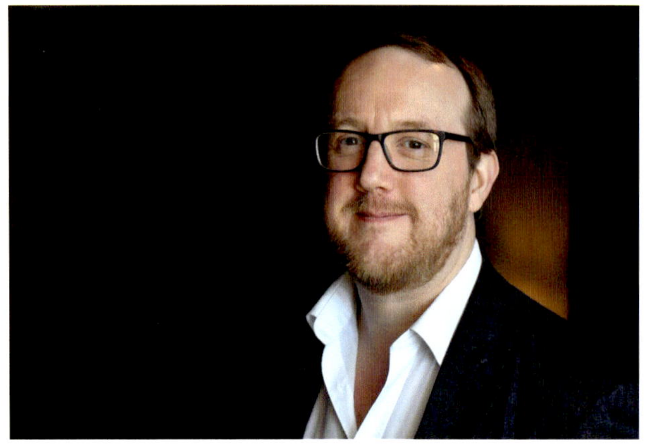

Mark Rees.
(Photo by Gayle Marsh)